MW01194682

How to Collect & Invest in
CHINA STAMPS

Richard Tang

"The World's Most Lucrative Collectibles Market"

Printed in the United States of America

Richard Tang

Contents

Richard Tang

Chapter 1
Introduction

A very warm welcome to the World of Philately! And thank you for picking up this book. I am delighted to be your tour guide on this journey. We are going to explore the most fascinating and dynamic arena of modern philately: China Postage Stamps!

By reading this book, you might probably belong to one of the following groups:

- An investor who has China stamps in your portfolio

- An intermediate to advanced China stamp collector

- A beginner China stamp collector

- A stamp collector who hasn't started collecting China stamps. You might or might not have the intention to venture into this area, but want to know more about it

- You are not, or yet to be, a China stamp collector/ investor but this topic has caught your attention; and you would like to find out more about it before going any further

No matter which group you belong to, I hope the information laid out herein will help you gain a closer insight and a systematic view of this topic.

You are now holding the color version of this book, which offers optimal visual impact for your research on this topic. The black and white version is also available in the market. It is definitely cheaper but with much less visual effectiveness.

Please note that the purpose of this book is not to provide any financial advice. You are solely responsible for any investment decision you make.

This book is not about China's postal history either, although it briefly summarizes the Chinese philatelic development, corresponding to the political and social changes in the country's history. It only aims to highlight different periods' well-sought-after philatelic issues.

This book will not replace any existing stamp catalogue out there. Again, it will just highlight the highly-demanded issues, in which value reference might be provided in certain parts of the book. If you are looking into details of each and every issue, a catalogue is still required.

Then, what is this book about? Let me summarize in a few points below:

- Why China stamps have become so popular over the last few decades?

- What are the highly sought-after China stamps?

- How to collect China stamps?

- How to sell China stamps?

- Whether to consider adding China stamps into your investment portfolio?

The information provided in this book is compiled from my 15 years of actively collecting China stamps, studying different catalogues, reading and researching, attending exhibitions and auctions, taking part in forums and social media groups and interacting with fellow collectors worldwide, many of whom have over 40 years of experience under their sleeves.

Before we go any further, let me share with you, especially those of you who are new to the hobby, some observations on stamp collecting in general.

Myths about Stamp Collecting

There are common beliefs about stamp collecting adopted by people all over the world, which might not be accurate in the modern context. Let's go through some of such myths:

Myth #1: Stamp collecting is a luxury hobby

It can't be denied that building a solid and valuable collection needs a lot of time and effort, and most importantly, money. But it doesn't mean you can't have a decent collection while being on budget.

If your area of interest is rarity and errors, you can't definitely avoid paying multiple thousands of dollars in auction to acquire your desired materials.

However, if you simply aim to build your collection around common topics, let's say sports, Elvis Presley, animals, landscape etc., you can easily find many beautiful stamps at affordable price.

It all depends on what you want. Just like all other hobbies, stamp collecting is not necessary a luxury one unless you want to be the owner of items with only a few examples known to exist or survive.

Myth #2: Old stamps are rare and expensive

Many novice collectors think so! But it is not true. Think about the first adhesive postage stamp in the world – The 1840 Penny Black! Millions of them are well-preserved until today. The price of this stamp ranges from a few hundred to a few thousand dollars, depending on the plate number and its condition. Since it is the first stamp in the world, demand is substantial.

How about the rest of the stamps issued during the same period? Are all of them worth hundreds or thousands of dollars? Not always the case, I'm afraid! So, next time if you come across a stamp dated 1870 listed for sale at only 50 cents, don't be surprised!

There is a commerce mobile app in Singapore called "Carousell". I have seen so many interesting stories related to stamps on this platform.

There are people who inherit a few old stamps from their parents or grandparents, and they believe that these are old and rare. They go ahead and list the stamps for sale at insane price. For example, someone was selling the <u>used</u> China Qing dynasty dragon coil stamp at $60!!! Some even listed a couple of Commonwealth low denomination King George V stamps at $100,000, simply because they are intoxicated by this myth #2.

That is another reason why I am writing this book, so that readers won't be lured by this stereotype and overpay for so-called "vintage stamps". I have ever seen a collector who believes that every China stamp is expensive. He used to spend thousands of dollars on a few PRC sets, which he can acquired at less than one third even at the catalogue value. He is not alone. So many novice collectors are overcharged nowadays.

So, if you are still thinking old stamps are very expensive, you might adopt a different point of view after reading this section.

Myth #3: Used stamps are more valuable than mint

A lot of people argued that a used stamp carries with it the journey of the letter, especially during the old time when transport was not that convenient, and postmen had to cross dangerous mountains and rivers, and even sites of warfare, to deliver it to the intended recipient.

It might be true if the stamp is still on envelop, on which the following information can be seen:

- ✓ Who are the sender and recipient; Whether they are significant figures of the history or just two random people

- ✓ The address of the sender and recipient

- ✓ The date the letter being sent and received

- ✓ Any special events related to the letter

- ✓ Whether the stamp on envelop is defined as error, or of rare variety, or being withdrawn shortly after issued. And so on...

If the used stamp is off paper, 90% of the time, it won't be priced as high as mint. Without seeing the details mentioned above, there is less history value being perceived. Many mint stamps are worth five to ten times compared to their used counterparts.

There are some special cases in which used stamps are more valuable than mint, for example:

- ✓ The stamp was issued but not many of them were postally used. They can be used for fiscal purposes. So, those with postal cancellation marks will just cost an arm and a leg

- ✓ The used stamp carried a special or uncommon type of postmark

Myth #4: Stamp collecting is an obsolete hobby

Stamp collecting became a hobby as soon as the 1840 Penny Black was issued. After 170 years, people are still collecting stamps.

About 40 years ago, the major hobby that was adopted by almost every school kids was stamp collecting. But today if you ask around, only one or two out of dozens of school kids would tell you that they are interested in stamps. Teenagers of 40 years ago can focus on collecting without any distractions from computer game or any other forms of entertainment like what we have today.

Does this make stamp collecting an obsolete hobby? Not really, I believe.

While it is true that stamp collecting is no longer a trend of the mass, it remains a hobby with growing collector base and higher level of specialization. Today's collectors, with better access to information and resources, tend to focus more on quality rather than quantity. The number of collectors with a random collection is shrinking. But the number of collectors with more specialized collection is on the rise. I have also seen many collectors of the previous generation, now with stable career and spending power, return to the hobby, rebuild the collection and take it to the next level. Some even educate and inspire their children to appreciate stamps.

Furthermore, governments, philatelic societies and postal organizations around the world have put enormous efforts to promote stamp collecting as a hobby. China government is a good example.

Thus, instead of becoming obsolete, stamp collecting just moves away from being a hobby of the mass.

Myth #5: Stamp collecting is dying out

Cutting-edge technology brought about tremendous changes in the global postage service. We no longer send as many mails as we used to. Yet millions of stamps are still being designed and issued around the world every single year. Certain portions of these go to collectors' stamp albums.

According to stamp dealers' observation, fewer people visit their shops compared to 20 years ago. Some said stamp collecting is on the verge of dying out. However, online commercial platforms, like eBay, witnessed a dramatic increase in the sales of stamps and other collectibles over the years. If you ever bid for stamps on eBay, you will encounter competing bids 90% of the time. Sometimes the competition is so fierce that the winning bid can be ten times more than your highest bid! Sounds familiar enough? People are still buying stamps! They just buy less from bricks-and-mortar stores thanks to the convenience of online shopping. In fact, many people said that without the Internet, they would never continue collecting.

Another observation is the shrinking membership of various philatelic societies. Take APS (The American Philatelic Society) as an example. The society's membership reached its peak during the late 1980s and 1990s, with over 55,000 members. To date, it has declined to 32,000. Does the number tell us something? The most obvious fact is that the society incurs a net loss of at least 20,000 members over the last 20 years.

This might reflect the number of Baby Boomer collectors who retired from the hobby. This, too, might reflect the number of collectors who move away from paid membership of offline societies to free membership of various online stamp forums, where they can discuss about their hobby and meet people of the same interest any time of the day, any day of the week!

In fact, many of the collectors that I've met, especially those from Generation Y onwards, never belong to any philatelic society. Yet, they actively collect stamps and their collections are often built with interesting concepts and solid quality.

If you have a chance to visit stamp shops on a frequently basis, especially in Singapore, Malaysia, Hong Kong and China, you might observe that they are busy most of the time and regular and new customers keep visiting those shop day in, day out.

Stamp collecting might be declining a little bit in First World countries. But it has been picking up rapidly in Asia, especially in China. We'll discuss about that in due time.

In conclusion, stamp collecting is not dying. It is just changing!

Recent Trends in Stamp Collecting

As mentioned above, while many stamp collectors are giving up the hobby, many are picking it up. This trend, along with modern technology, has brought the global landscape of stamp collecting to the next level. Some of the most wanted areas of modern philately include:

- British Commonwealth pre-1935 (Queen Victoria, King Edward VII and King George V)

- China stamps, especially People's Republic of China and Qing dynasty. Hong Kong and Macau is on the rise

- French Colonies

- USA, especially pre-1940 and mint

- Independent India

- South America

- Russia

- Eastern Europe during the 1945-1965 period

In general, mint stamps are usually in greater demand and yield higher value.

Most of the stamps issues after 1950 are of less demand because they are issued in millions and face less risk of being destroyed by wars. However, many issues of modern China stamps (including Hong Kong and Macau) are still highly sought after, mainly due to speculation during recent years.

A well-organized collection is usually valuated much more than a random one.

Significant price discrepancy can be observed between good and average condition of the same stamp.

Specialized/ topical/ thematic collections (such as Zodiac) are getting more and more popular. Yet the demand is still comparatively thin for the time being.

Forgeries are plenty in the market, especially for rare and highly demanded stamps. Some of them look just exactly the same as the original so that only cutting-edge technology can detect.

The Benefits of Stamp Collecting

Initially, most people would start collecting stamps as a pastime. Along the way, it will be fascinating enough to discover how much more they can derive from it instead of a mere hobby:

The knowledge: Collectors usually pay attention to the historical and social events, the figures, the landscape, the animals, the plants and the objects that are featured on the stamps, and even the currency that is used as denomination. They tend to do further research and acquire knowledge on the subject that they are interested in.

The soft skills: Stamp collecting can train you to become a more patient and detail-oriented person. Classifying and organizing stamps is an efficient way to improve your brain's capacity. Have you ever come across a stamp and you immediately recognize it is the missing piece that you're searching? Stamp collecting is just that powerful.

The pleasure: No collectors ever deny that stamps bring great relaxation and enjoyment. It may easily take you hours just to sit down and view your collection. Do you still recall the feeling of utmost satisfaction when you manage to find that particular stamp to complete your set?

The creativity: Stamp collecting has no rule. You can build your collection around whatever concept you come up with. There's so much fun to brainstorm on how to build a collection; and once it takes shape, imagine how awesome you feel, and how creative you discover you are!

The investment: Last but not least, although most of us start collecting without any monetary drive, would you be happy if one day you wake up and find your stamps is worth thousands of dollars? One of my fellow collectors bought 3 monkey stamps (T46) when it was issued in 1980, spending much less than a dollar back then. He just earned a few thousand bucks lately after selling two of them! Amazing, isn't it?

Basic Philatelic Terminologies

I would dedicate this section to those who are new to stamps. Advanced collectors please bear with me for a little while.

Stamp Condition

MNH – mint never hinged, or **MOG** – mint with original gum: A stamp that is in perfect condition as newly-issued in the post office.

MH – mint hinged: A mint stamp that was previously mounted onto a page of an old album, using a stamp hinge, which is a small, folded, transparent, rectangular piece of paper coated with a mild gum.

MNG – mint no gum: A mint stamp that was issued with no gum at the back, or with gum being washed off.

Used: A stamp that has been used postally or fiscally.

Cancellation: A mark applied on stamps to indicate that it has been used. There are postal cancellation and fiscal cancellation.

✓ Postal cancellation: applied when the stamp is postally used

✓ Fiscal cancellation: applied on both postage stamps and revenue stamps, when it is used for fiscal purposes

Cancelled to Order (CTO): The stamp is cancelled but not used postally. Most of the time, it will be sold to collectors.

Stamp Components

Denomination: Face value of the stamp at the time when it is issued.

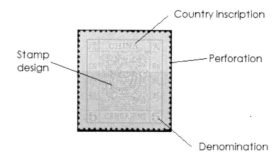

Gum: The material used on the back of the stamp to form an adhesive when it is wetted.

Perforation: Holes at the edges of the stamp so that it can be separated from a sheet.

Roulette: Perforations in the form of long cuts.

Imperforation: A stamp without holes at the edges. It needs to be cut using scissors to be separated from a sheet.

11

Margin: The space at the borders of the stamp. It can be blank, or can contain series number, issuing company, bar code, or some logos. Stamps with margins used to be highly sought after by collectors, but the trend has slowed down recently.

Gutter: The wide margin in between the stamps.

Perfin: A stamp that has initials or names perforated across its surface. Often used by commercial organizations as a security measure.

Watermark: The pattern which appears as various shades when viewed by transmitted light. Most of the earlier stamps bear with them different types of watermarks, usually observed on the back side of the stamp.

Common Types of Stamps

Commemorative: A stamp that is issued to commemorate an event, a person or an anniversary.

Definitive: A stamp that is part of a regular issue during different periods.

Bisect: A stamp which is cut in half, vertically, horizontally, and usually diagonally. Each of it equals to half of the face value. It is used when stamps of lower denomination are in short supply. Bisect usually cost a lot in the market nowadays.

Stamp sheet: A sheet that contains multiple stamps, usually of the same design.

Booklet: A folder with panes of stamps or sheets, issued by the postal authorities.

Coil Stamp: A stamp that is part of a long strip of many stamps, usually of similar design.

Se-tenant: Stamps that are joined together as issued, with different values and/or designs.

Miniature sheet (or **Souvenir sheet**): A small sheet of one or more stamps, with an ornamental border around showing additional decoration or information, issued for souvenir purposes.

Official stamp: A stamp that is issued for use by government departments, such as tax, military etc.

Overprint

Overprint: The additional print added to the original design of the stamp, such as a change in government, a change in postal rate, the use of a stamp in a different territory, or to denote a particular use (fiscal).

Surcharge: An overprint that alters the stamps face value. As in the example below, the original stamp was issued at 3 cent but surcharged at one cent.

Provisional: A stamp issued for temporary use to meet postal demands until new stocks can be obtained. The issuance of provisional stamps might be occasioned by a change in name or government, occupation of foreign territory, a change in postal rates, a change of currency, or the need to provide stamps that are in short supply.

Postage due: A stamp indicating that the postal fee has not been correctly paid and the sum due for the delivery of the item.

Airmail stamp: Used for postal articles carried by an aircraft.

Chapter 2
The Increasing Popularity of China Stamps

Many years back, stamp collecting was an extra-curricular activity of school kids around the world. Modern technology was thought to have killed this hobby due to the decrease in the usage and demand of postage stamps. Out of surprise, this turned out to be untrue. In Chapter 1, we have discussed that stamp collecting is not an obsolete hobby; and it is not really on the verge of dying out.

Statistics have shown that there are about 60 million stamp collectors around the world, one third of which come from China.

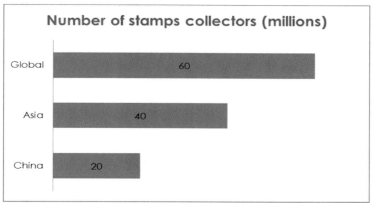

(Source: Stanley Gibbons, Barclays, ASDA)

Let's take a look at the key factors that drive the popularity of China stamps in the modern philately landscape.

1. The Role of China Economy

Based on the annual assessment by Forbes magazine, China has over 210 USD billionaires in 2015, only second to the United States in terms of ranking. Besides, there are many billionaires and millionaires who are Chinese descendants living in the North America, Singapore, Malaysia, Australia and European countries.

Like so much of the global economy these days, the center of the world's multi-billion-dollar stamp collecting market is shifting east.

Stamp collecting was banned under Mao's regime until 1976. In 2000, the China government made it an official policy to foster stamp collecting among youngsters. Wealthy Chinese are now beginning to buy back their heritage on a massive scale. Young Chinese investors are laughing their way to the bank with significant gains on their China stamp portfolio. Out of nowhere, Asian stamp collectors are turning a dying hobby into a high-end investment! Auction houses are sprouting up in Hong Kong, Singapore Shanghai and Beijing, driving many wealthy Chinese collectors jumping on the bandwagon.

In December 2015, the International Monetary Fund has approved the Chinese Yuan (CNY) into its elite reserve currency. With this policy, from October 2016 onwards, the CNY will join the USD, EUR, JPY and GBP in the list of currencies that IMF uses as an international reserve asset. This will definitely affect the purchasing power of the Chinese people, which in turns could affect the landscape of Chinese antiques and collectibles markets.

2. The Growth of Global Chinese Population

Mainland Chinese

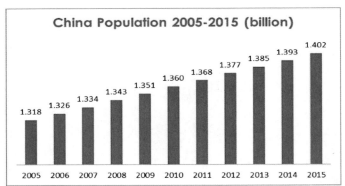

(Source: United Nations)

The sheer size of the Chinese population explains its large representation in the international philatelic community. With increasingly higher purchasing power and greater appetite for stamps, they are the key driver of this lucrative Oriental collectibles market.

The number of stamp collectors in China is still growing rapidly. Keith Heddle, Managing Director of Stanley Gibbons once said: "The Chinese are collecting in their millions. In China there is no stigma about collecting stamps – they want to reclaim their history." He added that this pool of 20 million collectors contribute $9 billion annually to the global stamp market.

In addition, China officially announced the end of its one child policy in October 2015, in an attempt to cope with its ageing population, imbalanced gender ratio and shrinking workforce. The change takes effect from January 2016, in which married couples are allowed to have a second child. The number of collectors is expected might increase even faster at least in the next 50 years, if China government sustains their current effort to promote stamp collecting.

Overseas Chinese

There are over 50 million overseas Chinese in the world. Most of them live in Southeast Asia. A few millions live in the US, Canada, Australia and Europe.

According to research papers by David Bartlett (1997) and Kazuo Fukuda (1998), overseas Chinese were estimated to control <u>$1.5-2 trillion</u> in liquid assets and have considerable amounts of wealth to stimulate economic power in China. This statistics is almost <u>20 years old</u> and the number was in trillions! Imagine how it could be nowadays.

This group also contributes significantly to the sales of China stamps all over the world. It's normal to see them spending five figures in auction.

According to my observation over the last 5 years, many of those who place bids for China stamps on eBay are overseas Chinese (by name*). They usually bid aggressively and sometimes drive the hammer price to an unimaginable figure!

> ** Nowadays, by looking at Chinese surname, you would probably know whether they are Mainland or overseas Chinese. Mainland people have their names romanized based on Pinyin system (for example, Mao Zedong), while non-Mainland Chinese have a multitude of romanization systems when it comes to names (Singapore: Lee Kuan Yew instead of Li Guangyao; Hong Kong: Chow Yun-fat instead of Zhou Runfa; Taiwan: Tsai Ing-wen instead of Cai Yingwen, etc.). Not to mention that most of overseas Chinese nowadays have a Christian name (Andy Lau, Stephanie Sun etc.)*

3. Non-Chinese Collectors Shifting to China Stamps

I once received an email from an American stamp collector with over 50 years of experience. He shared about his great interest in China stamps and how his fellow American collectors were shifting their attention to this area.

The figures of non-Chinese collectors are currently estimated based on membership of philatelic associations. Yet, there are many closet collectors who belong to no formal associations and are philateling in the privacy of their own homes. We could come across many of them in online forums and philatelic exhibitions. Many of them claim China stamps to be among their top focus. With the increasing popularity of China stamps, non-Chinese collectors globally will definitely jump on the bandwagon and claim their share in this lucrative area.

Nick Salter of Philatelic Investors shared that the Chinese appear to be buying as collectors, whereas Westerners are more likely to be buying for investment, in the anticipation that they can sell on into the Chinese market at a later date.

Stability and Sustainability

The hard truth is that China stamp market is still highly volatile. Prices spike and fall on a regular basis due to the presence of thousands of big dealers who hold very large stocks and have the power to manipulate the price. However, the value of China stamps is still on the rise in the medium to long term.

Dealers in Singapore can price China stamps at three times higher than the catalogue value; and collectors are still willing to pay the price. The used set of S38 Goldfish issues of 1960, for example, has an average catalogue value of $100. Yet some shops in Singapore are now selling it at S$350 (approximately $250). On a side note, sellers on Carousell (a Singapore-based marketplace mobile app) have never priced this set below S$150, at least at the time of this writing.

According to Mr. Tan Chun Lim, an expert in China stamps, owner of CS Philatelic stamp shop in Singapore, and editor of the CS China Stamp Catalogue, catalogue value can only be used as a reference. Buyers may pay much higher, depending on the demand. On the other hand, if you're lucky enough, you may grasp decent quality stamps at much lower price.

China Stamp Index

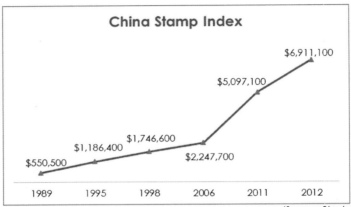

(Source: Stanley Gibbons)

Another interesting aspect to look at is the Stanley Gibbons China stamp index, which track the performance of 200 pieces of rare investment-grade China stamps since 1989.

Growth has been substantial, with cumulative growth of 1,170% over the last 25 years, and compound annual growth of 10.7%

Besides, collectors can also refer to the CN100 index, provided by the China Stamp Index Company Limited. The company was founded in 2011 by Mr. Ricky Tam – the Chairman of the Hong Kong Institute of Investors and Director of the World Federation of Investors Corporation, and Dr. Sam Chiu – the CEO of David Feldman Asia. Statistics also shows the steep uptrend. However, the index hasn't been updated since 2012.

Generally speaking, China stamp is an extraordinarily hot trend. If you have been collecting for years, congratulations! You might have started or will be gaining upon liquidation of your collection. If you would like to start venturing in this area but yet to do so, don't wait until the market goes wilder!

Chapter 3
An Overview of Chinese Philately

In this chapter, we'll take a closer look at the development of China philately through different periods of the history. Years of warfare and changes in political regimes contributed to the complexity of the Chinese postal history. As much as possible, we will use the standard Chinese Pinyin instead of the old Postal Romanization system for locations and Wade-Giles system for people, such as *Chongqing* (now) for *Chung King* (then), *Beijing* (now) for *Peking* (then), *Mao Zedong* (now) for *Mao Tse Tung* (then).

1. Qing Dynasty Stamps (1865 – 1912)

1.1 Local Municipal Posts of Treaty Ports

In 1863, a Municipal postal system was established in Shanghai. The first stamp of China was issues in 1865. After that, branch offices were opened subsequently in different Treaty Ports.

In this chapter, wherever possible, we'll count the number of stamp (by design) issued by each period and region.

- **Shanghai** (1865 – 1896): 32 issues, 189 stamps including surcharge and postage due, excluding errors and varieties. Inscription "Shanghai L.P.O." and "上海書信館" were displayed on the stamps, and later, "Shanghai Local Post", "Shanghai Municipal Local Post", "上海工部書信館"

- **Amoy** (1895 – 1896), now known as *Xiamen*: 9 issues, 35 stamps including surcharge and postage due, excluding errors and varieties. Inscription: "Amoy" and "廈門工部郵政局" (Amoy Post Office)

- **Chefoo** (1893 – 1896), now *Yantai*: 3 issues, 13 stamps, excluding errors and varieties. Inscription: "Chefoo"

- **Chinkiang** (1894 – 1895), now *Zhenjiang*: 8 issues, 55 stamps including surcharge, postage due and official, excluding errors and varieties. Inscription: "Chinkiang Postal Service" and "鎮江工部"

- **Chungking** (1893 – 1895), now *Chongqing*: 5 issues, 13 stamps including surcharge and postage due, excluding errors and varieties. Inscription: "Chungking L.P.O." and "重慶信局"

- **Foochow** (1895 – 1896), now *Fuzhou*: 3 issues, 11 stamps, excluding errors and varieties. Inscription: "Foochow"

- **Hankow** (1893 – 1897), now *Hankou*: 11 issues, 43 stamps including surcharge and postage due, excluding errors and varieties. Inscription: "Hankow L.P.O.", "Hankow Local Post" and "漢書信館"

- **Ichang** (1894 – 1896), now *Yichang*: 3 issues, 19 stamps including surcharge and postage due, excluding errors and varieties. Inscription: "Ichang", "宜昌(書)信館"

- **Kewkiang** (1894 – 1896), now *Jiujiang*: 6 issues, 42 stamps including surcharge and postage due, excluding errors and varieties. Inscription: "Kewkiang Local Post" and "九江(書信館,公務局)"

- **Nanking** (1896 – 1897), now *Nanjing*: 3 issues, 16 stamps, excluding errors and varieties. Inscription: "Nanking Local Post" and "金陵書信館" (Jinling Letter House)

- **Wei Hai Wei** (1898 – 1899), now *Weihai*: 2 issues, 4 stamps, excluding errors and varieties

- **Wuhu** (1894 – 1897): 9 issues, 105 stamps including surcharge and postage due, excluding errors and varieties. Inscription: "Wuhu Local Post" and "蕪湖", later "Wuhu China"

The map below illustrates the locations of the Treaty Ports'. Wei Hai Wei is, in fact, not a Treaty Port. But it is categorized in this group for collector convenience.

1.2 Chinese Imperial Post

The first stamp of the Imperial Customs Post was issued in 1878, under the reign of Emperor Guangxu (1875 – 1908). About 24 stamps were issued between 1878 and 1896, excluding errors and varieties. Inscription: "大清國郵政", "大清國郵政局" (Great Qing Postage), with the English word "China".

The Chinese Imperial Post Office was officially established in 1896, by Robert Hart (1835 – 1911). From 1896 to 1912, about 147 stamps were issued, including surcharge, postage due, provisional and express letter stamps, excluding errors and varieties. Inscription: "大清國郵政" and "Chinese Imperial Post" or "Imperial Chinese Post". The first commemorative stamps of China were issues under the reign of the Empror Xuantong (1908 – 1912), which shows "Chinese Empire" on its design.

There are also postage due stamps and express letter stamps issued during this period of time. For express letter stamps, see Chapter 4 for more details.

1.3 Formosa

1.3.1 Chinese Formosa

The first stamp was issued in 1886, when Taiwan became a province of China. Inscription: "Formosa" or "臺灣郵票" (Stamp of Taiwan).

The later stamps show "Formosa China" and "大清臺灣郵政局" (Great Qing Taiwan Postage), with various types of handstamp overprints.

1.3.2 Republic of Formosa

After the Sino-Japanese war, Formosa island was ceded to Japan. However, Tang Jingsong – the Governor of Formosa resisted the Japanese and proclaimed Taiwan an independent republic, known as the short-lived Republic of Formosa, or Black Flag Republic.

15 stamps were issued during this short period between May and October 1895, with the inscription "臺灣民主國" (Taiwan Democratic State).

1.4 Tibet

Imperial Chinese troop occupied Tibet in 1910. Dragon stamps of Qing dynasty were overprinted with English, Chinese and Tibetan scripts for use in Tibet. In 1912, Tibet became an independent state and Chinese post offices were closed.

2. Foreign Post Offices in China (1862 – 1922)

2.1 British Post Offices (1862 – 1921)

British postal facilities were set up in 16 Treaty Ports, including, Amoy (*Xiemen*), Anping (*Tainan*), Canton (*Guangzhou*), Chefoo (*Yantai*), Foochow (*Fuzhou*), Hankow (*Hankou*), Hoihow (*Haikou*), Ningpo (*Ningbo*), Shanghai, Swatow (*Shantou*), Tientsin (*Tianjin*) and Wei Hai Wei (*Weihai*).

Stamps of Hong Kong were used by these British post offices, cancelled by a postage mark specially designed for each location.

From 1917 to 1921, stamps of Hong Kong were overprinted with "China" for use in all these locations. These are known as the general issues.

2.2 French Post Offices (1894 – 1922)

Stamps of France were designed or overprinted with "Chine" in the inscription, for use in Amoy (*Xiemen*), Chefoo (*Yantai*), Foochow (*Fuzhou*), Hankow (*Hankou*), Ningpo (*Ningbo*), Peking (*Beijing*), Shanghai and Tientsin (*Tianjin*).

British	French	German

2.3 German Post Offices (1886 – 1919)

Stamps of Germany were overprinted with "China" for use in Amoy (*Xiemen*), Canton (*Guangzhou*), Futschau (*Fuzhou*), Hankau (*Hankou*), Itschang (*Yichang*), Nanking (*Nanjing*), Peking (*Beijing*), Shanghai, Shanhaikwan (*Shanhai Pass*), Swatau (*Shantou*), Tientsin (*Tianjin*), Tongku (*Tanggu*), Tschifu (*Yantai*), Tschinkiang (*Zhenjiang*), Tsinanfu (*Jinan*) and Weihsien (*Weixian*).

2.4 Indo-China Post Offices (1902 – 1919)

Stamps of Indo-China were overprinted with "Chine" as general issues. Different post offices also had their own individual issues. Below is the list of overprint types used by each office:

- ✓ "Pakhoi": in Beihai - Guangxi
- ✓ "Tchongking": in Chongqing
- ✓ "Canton" or "KoangTcheou" or "KoangTcheouWan": in Guangzhou
- ✓ "Hoi Hao": in Haikou – Hainan
- ✓ "YunnanFou" or "YunnanSen": in Kunming – Yunnan
- ✓ "Mongtze" or "MongTseu": Mengzi – Yunnan

2.5 Italian Post Offices (1917 – 1921)

Stamps of Italia were overprint with "Pechino" the use in Beijing, and "Tientsin" for the use in Tianjin.

2.6 Japanese Post Offices (1900 – 1921)

Stamps of Japan were overprinted with "支那" (Shina) for use in Chefoo (*Yantai*), Chinkiang (*Zhenjiang*), Foochow (*Fuzhou*), Hangchow (*Hangzhou*), Kiukiang (*Jiujiang*), Newchwang (*Yingkou*), Ningpo (*Ningbo*), Shasi (*Jingzhou*), Soochow (*Suzhou*) and Tianjin (*Tientsin*).

Japanese   Russian   US

2.7 Russian Post Offices (1899 – 1920)

Stamps of Russia were overprinted with "КитАй" (Cathay) for use in Chefoo (*Yantai*), Hankow (*Hankou*), Kalgan (*Zhangjiakou*), Peking (*Beijing*), Port Arthur and Danly (*Lushun & Dalian*), Shanghai, Tientsin (*Tianjin*) and Urga (*Ulan-Bator*).

2.8 United States Postal Agency (1919 – 1922)

US stamps were overprinted with "Shanghai China" for use on mails from the US Postal Agency in Shanghai to the US.

3. Non-Chinese Administrative Regions (1862 – 1999)

3.1 Japanese Formosa (1895 – 1945)

After Japan defeated the Republic of Formosa's troop in Tainan in 1895, the island became part of the Japanese Empire. Stamps of Japan were used until 1945, when the island was returned to the Republic of China government of Chiang Kai-shek.

3.2 British Hong Kong (1862 – 1997)

Hong Kong became a British Crown Colony in 1841, after the First Opium War between the British and the Qing government. The first stamp of Hong Kong was issued in 1862, with the profile of Queen Victoria. Hong Kong issued its own stamps with the inscription "Hong Kong" and "香港" until it was returned to China in 1997.

British Monarch stamps of Hong Kong

Stamps of Hong Kong were issued during different periods:

- Queen Victoria (1837 – 1900)
- King Edward VII (1901 – 1910)
- King George V (1910 – 1935)
- King George VI (1936 – 1952)
- Queen Elizabeth II (1952 until 1997)

3.3 Portuguese Macau (1884 – 1999)

Portuguese sovereignty of Macau was recognized by the Qing government in 1887. The first stamp of Macau was issued in 1884.

Stamps of Macau were issued during different periods:

- King Luis (1861 – 1889)
- King Carlos (1889 – 1908)
- King Manuel II (1908 – 1910)
- Portuguese Republic (1910 until 1999)

Stamps of Macau show the inscription "Macau" in the design, and later with "Republica Portuguesa" and "澳門".

3.4 German Kiaochow (1897 – 1922)

The Jiaozhou Bay (previously Kiaochow, or Kiautschou in German), located in Shandong province, was ceded to Germany in 1897.

Initially, stamps of Germany and German Post Offices in China were used in this area, cancelled with the "Tsintau" or "Tsingtau" postmark (meaning *Qingdao* in German).

There are also a few surcharge issues on stamps of German Post Offices in China. From 1901, designs of German colonial stamps were adopted, with "Kiautschou" inscription being included.

During WWI, the Japanese troop took over Qingdao in 1914. Shandong province was officially returned to China in 1922. German stamps were in use in Jiaozhou until 1918.

3.5 Independent Tibet (1912 – 1965)

Tibet became an independent state when the Qing dynasty collapsed after the Xinhai Revolution 1911. Locally-issued stamps were used until 1965, when Tibet became an autonomous region of the People's Republic of China.

4. Republic of China (1912 – 1949)

The Qing dynasty was overthrown after the Xinhai Revolution and the Republic was established. The Republic can be divided into two periods:

- Beiyang Government (1912 – 1928), started with the presidency of Yuan Shikai, followed by years of warlord. The capital of this government is in Beijing

- Nationalist Government (1928 – 1949), led by Chiang Kai-shek, with Nanjing being the capital

The inscription appeared on stamps of the Republic read "中華民國郵政". English inscription "Republic of China Postage" was included in a couple of initial issues of the regime.

Generally, we can categorize the stamps of this period into five groups:

- Definitive issues
- Commemorative issues
- Province restricted issues
- Surcharge issues
- Special issues

4.1 Definitive Issues

4.1.1 Junk, Reaper and Hall of Classics

These classic definitive stamps were issued between 1913 and 1933, with 3 different designs:

- Low values feature a junk
- Middle values feature a farmer reaping rice
- High values feature the Hall of Classics in Beijing

For simplicity, let's address them as the "Junk definitive".

There stamps were printed in 3 different series:

- London series, 1913
- First Beijing series, between 1914 and 1919. The designs were re-engraved
- Second Beijing series, redrawn, printed from 1923 to 1933

The difference among these series can be distinguished from details on their design. Most catalogues will indicate the differences, in which Chan catalogue is the best reference.

4.1.2 Sun Yat-sen

Sun Yat-sen definitives are the most popular series of classic Chinese stamps. There are 14 general issues produced between 1931 and 1949, one Northeast China issue, one Taiwan issue and many surcharge issues used by the Nationalists, the Japanese, the Communists and also for provincial restricted use.

Continuous inflation of the 1940s has driven the changes in China stamp denomination during this period, from a few dollars, to a few thousand and dozens of thousands.

4.1.3 Martyrs

There are 6 martyrs being depicted on the stamps of the Nationalist regime between 1931 and 1949:

- Chen Qimei (referred to as Chen Ying Shih in various catalogues, 1878 – 1916)
- Deng Keng (Teng Keng, 1886 – 1922)
- Huang Xing (Huang Hsing, 1874 – 1916)
- Liao Zhongkai (Liao Chung Kai, 1877 – 1925)
- Song Jiaoren (Sung Chiao Ren, 1892 – 1913)
- Zhu Zhixin (Chu Chih Hsin, 1885 – 1920)

Chen Qimei　　　　*Deng Keng*　　　　*Huang Xing*

Liao Zhongkai　　*Song Jiaoren*　　*Zhu Zhixin*

4.2 Commemorative Issues

There are 5 commemorative issues produced during the Beiyang period, 26 issues under the Nationalist government.

4.3 Provincial Restricted Issues

Because of the significant difference between the local currencies and the national currency, stamps were issued or overprinted for special use in some provinces.

4.3.1 Taiwan

Between 1945 and 1949, stamps are designed with inscription "臺灣貼用" or overprinted with "限臺灣(省)貼用" (Restricted for use in (the province of) Taiwan) were issued in Taiwan.

During this period, Taiwan had two main issues and a postage due issue adopting the design of Nationalist stamps, and one Sun Yat-sen issue with unique design.

Overprints were applied on Nationalist Sun Yat-sen and Martyr stamps. Initially, some were overprinted on Japanese stamps.

4.3.2 Northeast China

In 1927, the junk definitive were overprinted with "限吉黑貼用" (Restricted for use in Jilin and Heilongjiang) and issued in Northeast China provinces. From 1928 to 1929, overprints were applied on Beiyang's Zhang Zuolin issue, Nationalist's unification issue (depicting Chiang Kai-shek) and Sun Yat-sen Mausoleum issue.

After the Japanese's surrender in 1945, new surcharge issues were overprinted with "限東北貼用" (Restricted for use in the Northeast). There was also a unique Sun Yat-sen issue produced in this region.

4.3.3 Xinjiang (Sinkiang)

Various stamps were overprinted for special use in Xinjiang from 1915 to 1949.

Surcharge "限新省貼用" (Restricted for use in Xinjiang province) was applied on the junk definitive, various commemorative issues, such as Beiyang's Zhang Zuolin issue, Nationalist's unification issue, Sun Yat-sen Mausoleum issue, as well as Sun Yat-sen and Martyr stamps.

4.3.4 Sichuan (Szechuan)

Stamps overprinted with "限四川貼用" (Restricted for use in Sichuan province) from 1933 to 1934, on Sun Yat-sen and Martyr stamps. Only 22 stamps are known to exist.

4.3.5 Yunnan

Stamps overprinted with "限滇省貼用" (Restricted for use in Dian province) from 1926 to 1934. Surcharge was applied on the junk series, Nationalist's unification issue, Sun Yat-sen Mausoleum issue, Tan Yankai issue, Sun Yat-sen and Martyr stamps.

4.4 Surcharge Issues

4.4.1 Provisional Surcharge (1912)

While waiting for the official stamps to be produced after the Republic was founded, surcharge was applied on Imperial stamps. Surcharge type: "中華民國" (Republic of China) and/or "臨時中立" (Provisional neutrality).

4.4.2 Anti-Bandit Overprint

During the early years of the Republic, there was social turmoil across the country. Bandits robbed not only treasures, but also postage stamps. Traders also brought stamps from areas with weaker currency to sell in those with stronger currency. These two factors caused great loss to the postal authorities.

To cope with this problem, local post offices were allowed to seal their stamps with local overprints, mostly with the name of the district. Overprints were mostly applied on the dollar value of Sun Yat-sen stamps and the Hall of Classics stamps. Some Martyrs stamps were also used.

Below is the list of overprint types that are known to exist:

- Gansu
  - Huining: 會甯
  - Jingyuan: 靖遠
  - Minxian: 岷縣
  - Pingliang: 平涼
  - Qin'an: 秦安
  - Tianshui: 天水
  - Wuwei: 武威
  - Xiahe: 夏河
  - Xining: 西寧
  - Yongchang: 永昌
  - Yongdeng: 永登
- Guangxi – Naning: 南寧
- Guizhou
  - Anshun: 安順
  - Bijie: 畢節
- Heilongjiang – Inner Manzhouli: 滿洲里
- Henan – Xincai: 新蔡
- Hunan
  - Hezhou: 河州
  - Ningxiang: 寧鄉
- Jilin – Tailaiqi: 泰來氣 or 泰來
- Qinghai
  - Huangyuan: 湟源
  - Xining: 西甯
  - Xining + Guide: 西甯，貴德
- Shaanxi
  - Jingyang: 涇陽
  - Xixiang: 西鄉
  - Tongzhou: 同州
- Sichuan
  - Baisha: 白沙
  - Central Xingchang: 中興場
  - Chengdu: 成都
  - Chongqing: 重慶
  - Daningchang: 大寧廠
  - Daxian: 達縣
  - East Sichuan: 東川
  - Fengjie: 奉節
  - Guanxian: 灌縣
  - Hechuan: 合川
  - Hejiang: 合江
  - Kaixian: 開縣
  - Kangding: 康定
  - Leshan: 樂山
  - Luxian: 瀘縣
  - Mianyang: 綿陽
  - Nanchong: 南充
  - Neijiang: 內江
  - North Beichang: 北碚場
  - Rongchang: 榮昌

- o Santai: 三台
- o Shaping: 沙坪
- o Shizhu: 石柱
- o Songgai: 松溉
- o Tongjiang: 通江
- o West Jietuo: 西界沱
- o Wutongqiao: 五通橋
- o Yibin: 宜賓
- o Yunyang: 雲陽
- o Zhongba: 中壩
- o Ziliujing: 自流井
- Xinjiang – Jitai: 奇台
- Yunnan
  - o Mengzi: 蒙自
  - o Mohei: 磨黑

4.4.3 Provincial Surcharge during the War (1941 – 1945)

Due to the alterations in postal rate during the war against Japan, various Sun Yat-sen stamps were surcharges for use in 20 different provinces. The most common overprint appeared on such stamps were "暫作" (Temporary for) and "改作" (Converted to).

4.4.4 Northeast Local Surcharge after the War (1945 – 1947)

When Manchukuo was dissolved towards the end of WWII, various local stamps of Manchukuo were overprinted for temporary use. Overprint shows "中華民國" (Republic of China) or "中華暫用" (China, temporary use).

Dr. Chan Shiu Hon (1920 – 2014), editor of the renowned Chan catalogue, classified the stamps into 4 categories:

- Authorized overprints: The surcharge pattern (chop) was made by the General Post Office and overprinted by local post offices

- Local overprints: The surcharge pattern was made and overprinted by the local post offices

- Requested overprints: The chop was made by speculators, but overprinted by the post offices upon being requested by these speculators

- Private overprints: Usually made by stamp dealers. These overprint types are mostly unusual. Stamps were sold to collectors, who have no idea whether the overprint is genuine

For further details of this specialization, please refer to the Chan catalogue.

4.4.5 Chinese Nationalist Currency Surcharge (1945 – 1948)

Since inflation was getting out of control after the war, stocks of old stamps were surcharged with new denomination, showing "國幣" inscription (Chinese Nationalist Currency) so that their value became valid. Surcharge was mostly applied on Sun Yat-sen and Martyr stamps.

4.4.6 Gold Yuan Surcharge (1948)

In August 1948, the Gold Yuan was introduced with the aim to cope with hyperinflation. Obsolete stocks of stamps were overprinted with "金圓". Since the currency wasn't backed by gold, inflation was getting even worse after that.

4.4.7 Silver Yuan Surcharge (1949)

The Gold Yuan collapsed in May 1949 and was replaced by the Silver Yuan. The Silver Yuan surcharge was applied on stamps separately in different provinces.

4.5 Stamps for Special Use

Postage Due: Between 1912 and 1949, the Republic of China produced 7 Postage Due issues, along with one surcharge issue applied on Imperial Chinese stamps, two surcharge issues applied on Sun Yat-sen stamps, one restricted issue in Northeast China, three restricted issues in Taiwan.

Postage Due, Parcels Post and Airmail stamps

Airmail: 6 Airmail issues were produced from 1921 to 1949, two out of which were surcharged due to currency value change. Various Airmail surcharges were applied for use in different provinces in 1949. There were 2 restricted issues for Xinjiang province, one overprinted on junk series, and one on Nationalist Airmail stamps.

Parcels Post: Stamps sold for mails that are too heavy for normal letter post. There were 3 parcel post issues from 1944 to 1947, one Gold Yuan surcharge issue in 1948, two restricted issues for Northeast provinces in 1948.

Express Letter stamp: One was issued in 1941 and various stamps were surcharged for use in different provinces during the Silver Yuan era.

Registration stamp: One was issued in 1941 and various stamps were surcharged for use in different provinces during the Silver Yuan era.

Relief Fund: Stamps sold for fund raising, usually for charity purposes. Stamps for war refugees relief fund were issued in 1944, and tuberculosis relief fund were issued in 1948.

Postage rate

Fund raising for charitable causes

Military Field Post: Stamps sold for use on soldier's correspondence and usually priced below postal rate. One issue was design for military use in 1945, the rest were overprinted on Nationalist stamps, with "軍郵" inscription (Military Stamp).

Unit Stamp: In 1949, inflation rate continued to escalate and the Gold Yuan stamps could not keep pace with the postal rates. Unit stamps were introduced without denomination to serve the postal needs at spot rates. These stamps were subsequently surcharged by both People's Republic of China and Taiwan for postal use after 1949.

Ordinary mail   *Airmail*   *Express mail*   *Registered mail*

5. Japanese Controlled Areas (1932 – 1945)

5.1 Manchukuo (1932 – 1945)

Manchukuo was formed by the Japanese in 1932, with Emperor Puyi being installed as the Head of State. It covers four provinces: Fengtien (*Liaoning*), Kirin (*Jilin*), Heilungkiang (*Heilongjiang*) and Jehol (*Rehe*).

Manchukuo stamps were produced to cater for the postal need of over 40 million people, and were inscribed with "滿洲國郵政" (Manchuria State Postage) and later, "滿洲帝國郵政" (Manchuria Empire Postage).

The Nationalist government, on the other hand, didn't recognize the existence of Manchukuo as an official state. As a result, all mails dispatched from Manchukuo to any parts of China were initially destroyed by mail clerks. This led to the introduction of China mail issues without the Manchukuo inscription, so that mails to China could be accepted.

The short-lived state issued about 169 stamps. Errors and varieties can be widely found due to the stamps being issued under wartime conditions. The state was dissolved in 1945, when Japan surrendered to the Allies.

5.2 Japanese Occupation of China (1941 – 1945)

In 1937, Japanese troops started their conquest over China. Stamps of the Republic of China, mostly Sun Yat-sen and Martyr issues, were overprinted for use in the areas controlled by the Japanese. Different overprints were produced in different areas:

- Kwangtung (*Guangdong*): "粵省貼用" (Restricted for use in Guangdong province)

- Mengkiang (*Mengjiang*): "蒙疆"

- North China: General issues with "華北", and various local issues, including:

    o Hopeh (*Hebei*): "河北"
    o Honan (*Henan*): "河南"

- o Shantung (*Shandong*): "山東"
- o Shansi (*Shanxi*): "山西"
- o Supeh (*Subei*): "蘇北"

- Nanking (*Nanjing*) and Shanghai's overprint patterns don't show the city names. Instead, we'll usually see "暫售" (Temporary sale) and "改作" (Converted to).

Besides, there are 4 official issues in Mengjiang (unique designs without overprints), 2 in North China districts and 2 in Nanjing/ Shanghai.

6. Communist China (1930 – 1949)

6.1 Early Communist China

The Chinese Communist Party was established in 1921. The Communists used to dominate Kuomintang's left wing until they were completely wiped out by Chiang Kai-shek in 1927. Those early days were tough for the Red Army, led by Mao Zedong. They set base in Jiangxi province's Jingang Mountains to gradually grow their forces and expand their territory.

6.1.1 Initial Communist Issues (1930 – 1932)

The first few stamps issued by the Communists are known as Red Posts issues, bearing the "赤色郵票" inscription (Red color stamps).

6.1.2 Chinese Soviet Republic (1931 – 1936)

The Chinese Soviet Republic was established in 1931, in the areas controlled by the Chinese Communist Party. Mao Zedong was elected the President of the Republic.

About less than 30 stamps were produced during this period, initially showing the "蘇維埃郵政" inscription (Soviet Postage), and later "中華郵政" (Chinese Postage).

Between 1931 and 1936, various battles took place between the Red Army and the Kuomintang forces. By 1936, the Communist headquarters was relocated to Yan'an, Shaanxi.

6.2 Liberated Areas (1937 – 1949)

In 1937, the two parties collaborated to tackle Japanese invasion during the Second Sino-Japanese War, following which their conflict resumed and escalated to a national scale Civil War until the Kuomintang was totally defeated in 1949.

During this period, the Communists issued stamps to meet the postal need in the regions they controlled, known as Liberated Areas. This section takes a closer look at that particular period. This is one of the most complex eras of Chinese philately.

6.2.1 Regional Issues

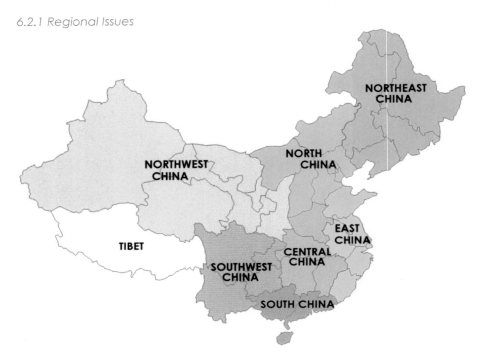

Central Plains Postal Administration: 3 official issues and various surcharge issues. About 44 stamps (designs) are known to exist. Stamps were inscribed "中華郵政中原區" (Chinese Postage, Central Plains Area) or "中州郵政" (Central Plains Postage). Overprint shows "中原解放區" (Central Plains Liberated Area) or "中州幣" (Central Plains Currency), applied on Nationalist Sun Yat-sen stamps, North China People's Post stamps and also on this region's issues.

East China People's Post: 7 official issues and various surcharge issues. About 83 stamps. Stamps were inscribed "華東郵政" (East China Post) or "華東人民郵政" (East China People's Post). Overprint shows "華東郵政", or "中華人民郵政華東區" (Chinese People's Post, East China region). Surcharge was applied on the region's issues, Nationalist Sun Yat-sen and parcel stamps.

North China People's Post: 7 official issues and various surcharge issues. About 102 stamps. Inscription and overprint show "華北人民郵政" (North China People's Post). Surcharge was applied on Sun Yat-sen and North China's local issues.

Northeast China People's Post: 39 official issues and various surcharge issues. 186 stamps including PRC's C and S issues. Surcharge was applied on the region's own issues, mostly for alteration of denomination. The word "東北" (Northeast) appears on stamp inscription.

Northwest China People's Post: One official issue with 4 stamps inscribed "西北人民郵政" (Northwest People's Post).

South China: One official issue and various surcharge applied on Sun Yat-sen stamps, unit stamps and on the region's own issue. About 26 stamps. Stamps were inscribed "華南郵政" (South China Postage).

Southwest China People's Post: 2 official issues and various surcharge applied on the region's own issue. Stamps were inscribed "中華人民郵政西南區" (Chinese People's Post, Southwest region). About 25 stamps including surcharge.

6.2.2 Local Issues

Central China

- <u>Henan:</u> Various surcharge issues. 27 stamps. Surcharge was mostly applied on Hubei stamps and Central Plains' regional stamps. Overprint shows "人民幣, 河南省" (People's Currency, Henan province)

- <u>Hubei:</u> About 4 official issues and various surcharge issues. 72 stamps including surcharge. Stamps were inscribed "中華郵政華中區" (Chinese Post, Central China Area). Surcharge was applied on Sun Yat-sen stamps. Overprint shows "華中郵政, 暫用" (Central China Post, temporary use)

- <u>Jiangxi:</u> Various surcharge issues. 41 stamps. Surcharge was applied on various Nationalist stamps. Overprint shows "人民郵政, 江西" (People's Post, Jiangxi)

East China

- <u>Bohai:</u> 4 issues. 15 stamps including surcharge. Stamps were inscribed "華東解放區" (East China Liberated Area)

- <u>Central Anhui:</u> Only one stamp, being surcharged on Huainan's issue

- <u>Central Jiangsu:</u> One official issue and various surcharge applied on this official issue, about 35 stamps, inscribed "Shuzhung"

- <u>Huainan:</u> One official issue and various surcharge applied on this issue, 31 stamps including surcharge. Inscription and overprint (if any) shows "Xuai Nan"

- <u>Jiaodong:</u> About 16 stamps, which were surcharged on Shandong's issues. Overprint shows "膠東" (Jiaodong)

- <u>Jiangsu:</u> 5 surcharge stamps applied on Nationalist Sun Yat-sen issues, showing "華東郵政，京" (East China Post, Jing)

- <u>Jiangsu-Anhui Border Area:</u> 4 official issues and various surcharge applied on its local issues and Huainan issues. Overprint shows "Xuazhung" or "華中解放區" (Central China Liberated Area*)

* Geographically, this area is in the east of China. However, the local post of that period might have a different categorization.

- <u>North Anhui:</u> 2 official issues and various surcharge applied on these issues. About 10 stamps, inscribed "華東江淮郵政" (East China Jianghuai Post) or "華東解放區" (East China Liberated Area)

- <u>Shandong:</u> 12 official issues and various surcharge issues. 144 stamps including surcharge. Stamps were inscribed "山東(省)戰時郵局" (Wartime Post Office of Shandong (Province)) or "山東郵政" (Shandong Postage). Overprint also shows "山東郵政"

- <u>South Anhui:</u> 10 stamps surcharged on Nationalist revenue stamps and Sun Yat-sen issues

- <u>West Anhui:</u> 4 stamps with hand-stamped surcharge on Nationalist revenue issues. Overprint shows "鳳台" (Fengtai)

- <u>Yanfu:</u> Mostly surcharge on Huainan issues. About 22 stamps, showing "Jan fu" or "Jan fu ky"

- <u>Zhejiang:</u> 6 designs with surcharge on Sun Yat-sen stamps. Overprint shows "華東郵政，杭" (East China Post, Hang)

North China

- <u>East Hebei:</u> One official issue and various surcharge showing "冀東(區)" (East Ji (Area)). 69 stamps in total

- <u>Hebei:</u> 17 stamps, all surcharged on Nationalist money order stamps and parcel stamps. Most of the surcharge show "**華北郵電**" (North China Post)

- <u>Hebei-Shandong-Henan Border Area:</u> 2 issues, 4 stamps inscribed "冀魯豫邊區" (Ji-Lu-Yu Border Area)

- <u>North-West Shanxi:</u> Only one stamp surcharged on Shanxi-Suiyuan's issues

- <u>Shanxi-Chahar-Hebei Border Area:</u> 7 official issues and various surcharge applied on these issues, or on Nationalist Sun Yat-sen stamps. About 67 stamps, including surcharge and imperforated varieties, inscribed "晋察冀邊區" (Jin-Cha-Ji Border Area). Overprint shows "晋察冀"

- <u>Shanxi-Hebei-Shandong-Henan Border Area:</u> 8 official issues and various hand-stamped surcharges on these issues. About 70 stamps inscribed "晋冀魯豫邊區" (Jin-Ji-Lu-Yu Border Area)

- <u>Shanxi-Suiyuan Border Area:</u> 3 official issues and various surcharge applied on these issues. 45 stamps, inscribed "晋綏郵政" (Ji-Sui Postage)

- <u>South Hebei:</u> Only 2 stamps being surcharged on Shanxi-Hebei-Shandong-Henan's Mao Zedong issue

- <u>South Shanxi:</u> 3 stamps, surcharged on Nationalist issues. Overprint shows "晋南人民郵政" (South Ji People's Post)

- <u>Suiyuan-Inner Mongolia Border Area:</u> 5 stamps, all surcharged on Shanxi-Suiyuan's issues

Northeast China

- <u>Andong:</u> One official issue, inscribed "遼東郵政" (Liaodong Postage) and various surcharge applied on this issue. Altogether 30 stamps including surcharge

- <u>Harbin:</u> 8 stamps, all surcharged on Nationalist Sun Yat-sen issues. Overprint shows "勝利紀念" (Victory Commemoration) or "雙十紀念" (10th October Commemoration)

- <u>Heilongjiang:</u> 4 stamps, all surcharged on Nationalist Sun Yat-sen issues. Overprint shows "勝利紀念" (Victory Commemoration)

- <u>Liaoning:</u> One official issue inscribed "中國解放區，遼寧郵政" (Chinese Liberated Area, Liaoning Postage), and various surcharge applied on Northeast China People's Post issues. 11 stamps in total

- <u>Port Arthur and Dairen:</u> Now *Lushun* & *Dalian*. 9 official issues and various surcharge applied on Japanese stamps, Manchukuo stamps and local issues. 72 stamps including surcharge. Overprint shows "遼寧郵政" (Liaoning Postage) or "關東郵政" (East Dalian Postage)

- <u>Ximan:</u> West Manchuria area. 3 official issues and 1 surcharge issues. 7 stamps in total, inscribed "中華郵政" (Chinese Postage) or "中華郵票" (Postage Stamp of China)

Northwest China

- <u>Gansu:</u> Two stamps, surcharged on Nationalist stamps, showing "人民郵政，隴南" (People's Post, Longnan)

- <u>Gansu-Ningxia-Qinghai Border Area:</u> 16 stamps surcharged on Nationalist issues, showing "人民郵政，甘" (People's Post, Gan)

- <u>Ningxia:</u> 4 stamps, surcharged on Nationalist stamps

- <u>North Shaanxi:</u> Only one stamp, surcharged on Shaanxi-Gansu-Ningxia's issue. Overprint shows "北陝" (North Shaanxi)

- <u>Shaanxi:</u> 14 stamps, surcharged on Nationalist issues. Overprint shows "人民郵政，陝(西)" (People's Post, Shaan(xi))

- <u>Shaanxi-Gansu-Ningxia Border Area:</u> 4 official issues, inscribed "陝甘寧邊區" (Shaan-Gan-Ning Border Area), and various surcharge applied on the local issues. 31 stamps in total

- <u>South Shaanxi:</u> Two official issues with 8 stamps, inscribed "人民郵政，陝南區" (People's Post, South Shaanxi)

- <u>Xinjiang:</u> 14 stamps, surcharged on Nationalist issues. Overprint shows "人民郵政，新" (People's Post, Xin)

- <u>Yili Republic:</u> An independent state in Xinjiang, established in 1945. This state produced 2 official issues and a surcharge issue applied on the main issues. 14 stamps in total. The Republic joined the People's Republic of China in 1949

Southwest China

- <u>East Sichuan:</u> 9 stamps, all surcharged on Southwest People's Post stamps. Overprint shows "東川" (East Sichuan)

- <u>Guizhan:</u> 8 stamps, all surcharged on Nationalist issues. Overprint shows "人民郵政，黔區" (People's Post, Qian)

- <u>West Sichuan:</u> 13 stamps, surcharged on Southwest People's Post stamps. Overprint shows "西川" (West Sichuan) or "人民郵政，蓉" (People's Post, Rong)

- <u>Yunnan:</u> 9 stamps, all surcharge on Nationalist unit stamps and Southwest People's Post stamps. Overprint shows "人民郵政，西南" (People's Post, Southwest)

7. People's Republic of China (1949 – Present)

Stamps of the People's Republic of China carry the inscription that reads "中國人民郵政" (Chinese People's postage) until 1957, when it was replaced by the simplified Chinese Characters with the same meaning "中国人民邮政".

From 1992 onwards, the inscription was shortened to "中国邮政", adding the English word "China" into the design.

7.1 C-Headed Issues (纪)

124 sets were issued between October 1949 and April 1967, numbered from C1 to C124, with a total of 406 stamps and 9 miniature sheets. Similar designs of C1 to C8 were used for Northeast province issues, denoted C1NE to C8NE. Reprints exist for C1 to C13 issues and C1NE to C8NE issues.

The left footer of each stamp shows the issue number, for example 纪12 (for C12), followed by two digits, the first of which indicates the number of stamps in the issue, and the second indicates the order of the stamp in the set.

In the example above, we see "纪109.3 –2". We can tell that this set is called C109. It has 3 stamps, and the stamp in the picture is the second stamp in the set.

7.2 S-Headed Issues (特)

75 sets were issued between October 1951 to 1966, numbered from S1 to S75, with a total of 444 stamps and one miniature sheet. Reprint exists for S1 to S4 issues.

Same information can be derived when we look at the left footer of the stamps.

7.3 W-Headed Issues

19 sets were issued between 1967 and 1970, numbered from W1 to W19, with a total of 80 stamps. These stamps were issued without index numbers.

One issue was withdrawn from sales, later known as the infamous "The whole country is red". Three other sets were prepared but not issued.

7.4 Numbered Issues

21 sets were issued between August 1970 and December 1974, with 95 stamps numbered from 1 to 95.

7.5 J-Headed Issues

185 sets were issued between May 1974 and Nov 1991, numbered from J1 to J185, with a total of 422 stamps and 18 miniature sheets

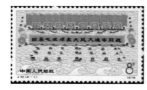 

7.6 T-Headed Issues

168 sets were issued between January 1974 and November 1991, numbered from T1 to T168, with a total of 696 stamps and 30 miniature sheets.

7.7 Year Issues (1992 – Present)

From 1992 onwards, commemorative and special issues were numbered with the following format: *Year – Set number in sequence*

An average of 20 to 30 sets has been issued every year. Later issues (2002 onwards) come with serial numbers that can be seen under ultraviolet light. This is among the efforts to prevent counterfeits due to the increasing popularity of China stamps in the market.

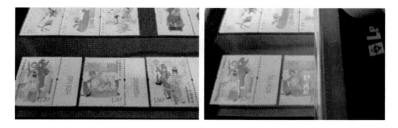

7.8 China Hong Kong (1997 – Present)

After Hong Kong was handed over to China, all stamps bear the inscription "Hong Kong China – 中国香港".

7.9 China Macau (1999 – Present)

Following the sovereignty transfer over Macau to China, stamps show the inscription "Macau China – 中国澳门".

7.10 Definitive Issues

There are 36 issues numbered from R1 to R32, RW, RN1, RN2 and RLd, including:

- 7 series featuring the Tian'anmen Square
- 4 series featuring the Revolutionary Monuments
- 4 series featuring Chinese folk houses
- 2 series featuring the Great Wall
- and other themes

7.11 Postage Due

There are 2 sets of Postage Due stamps, labeled D1 and D2, 14 stamps in total.

7.12 Airmail

There are 2 sets of Airmail stamps, labeled A1 and A2, 9 stamps in total.

7.13 Military Stamps

There are 2 sets of Military stamps, labeled M1 and M2, 4 stamps in total.

7.14 Surcharge Issues

There are 10 surcharge issues applied on Nationalist Sun Yat-sen stamps, unit stamps, East China Liberated Area's issues and money order stamps. Overprint shows "中國人民郵政" (China People's Post).

8. Republic of China (1949 – Present)

Stamps of the Republic of China after 1949 (Taiwan) are inscribed "中華民國郵政 – Republic of China" (Republic of China Postage), then later changed to "中華民國郵票 – Republic of China" (Stamp of the Republic of China), without any year or index number shown on the stamp.

The state also issued a number of Commemorative and Definitive stamps, Postage Due and Airmail stamps, and various surcharge issues.

From 2007 onwards, the inscription changed to "中華民國郵票 – Republic of China (Taiwan)" or only "臺灣 – Taiwan".

Summary: Timeline of Chinese Philately Development

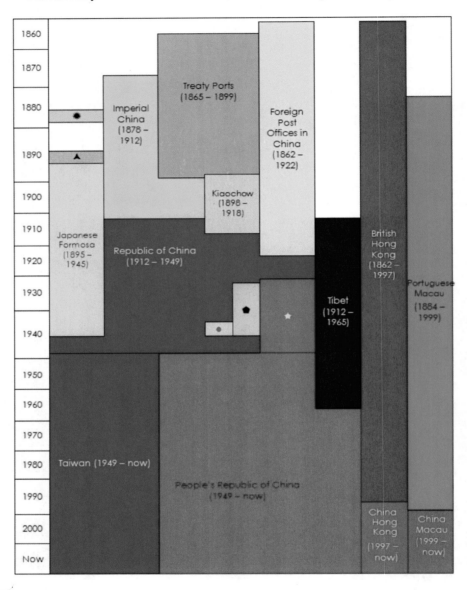

(✳) Chinese Formosa (1886 – 1888) (▲) Republic of Formosa (1895)
(●) Japanese Occupation (1941 – 1945) (⬟) Manchukuo (1932 – 1945)
(⭐) Early Communist China & Liberated Areas (1930 – 1949)

Chapter 4
The Highlights of China Stamps

This chapter will give an in-depth examination of the well-sought-after China stamps, some of which are rare and yielded extremely high price in auctions. This will give you an idea of what to look out for, while keeping your budget under control, and freeing yourself from being overloaded by too many choices in the market.

A. Qing Dynasty Period (Up to 1912)

The popularity of Qing dynasty stamps has been on the rise over the last few decades.

::: Treaty Ports :::

The imperforated stamps of Shanghai Treaty Port during the year 1865-1866, the first stamps of China, are rare and very expensive. Those using the "Candareen" currency usually fetch hundreds or thousands of dollars in the retail market or during dealer's auctions. For this type, used stamps are more valuable than mint.

There are a lot of forgeries of this type in the market. Two most obvious ways to identify the fake stamps are:

- Compare the English denomination and the Chinese denomination. Sometimes the English says "6" but the Chinese says "兩" (2)

- Count the number of "sticks" on the dragon's beard. If there are 7 sticks, high chance that the stamp is genuine

Other expensive examples of Treaty Ports are those issued in Wei Hai Wei. The scarlet stamp with handwritten denomination is worth thousands of dollars, whilst those with numbers on the design are worth in hundreds.

Collectors can acquire stamps issued by the rest of the Treaty Ports' at a quite reasonable price.

::: Imperial China :::

Qing dynasty stamps have always had its Large Dragon issues topping the price list, ranging from hundreds to thousands of dollars. Most of the time, mint examples fetch higher price.

The Small Dragon stamps, on the other hand, are much lower in value. Although their price currently stops at two to three digits, this type of stamps is still aggressively hunted by collectors worldwide.

The next issue that we should pay attention to is the Dowager birthday commemoration set of 1894. There are 9 stamps in the sets that cost a few thousands to acquire, whether they are mint or used. These stamps are quite difficult to preserve since it is easy to fade when exposed to moisture. Don't pay too high for those stamps that have been more or less "washed away".

There are two printings for this series: the first printing with thick yellow gum, and the second with thin and white gum.

In 1897, old stocks of stamps were surcharged with new currency. The stamps look like the following examples:

Some of these stamps are worth six digits in value, for example:

10 cents on 12 candarins brown orange (second print): *This stamp is estimated at $120,000-150,000. It is one of the rarest Imperial China stamps. Less than 12 mint copies of this stamp are known to exist today.*

2 cents on 2 candarins green (third print) *A block of 4 stamps vertically imperforated once realized closed to $90,000 in auction. Only about ten remaining of such pairs survive only block of four stamps with vertical imperforation known to exist. The individual stamp is currently listed over $300,000 in different catalogues.*

$1 on 3 cents deep red (third print): *The stamp was surcharged on a revenue stamp. This should not be mistaken with the same stamp with a wider "當壹圓" ($1) surcharge. Only 50 pieces of this type were produced and soon replaced with the bigger "當壹圓" type. To date, only 32 copies are known to be in existence. It used to fetch over $300,000 in auctions. Current value of the stamp across catalogues is more than $700,000.*

The later issues of the Qing dynasty are quite common and not very costly to collect. There are 6 common types:

* The dragon: Two types. Denomination between 0.5 cent to 10 cents

* The carp: Two types. Between 20 cents and 50 cents

* The flying bean goose: Two types. All on the dollar values ($1, $2 and $5)

The dragon and the carp stamps do not cost that much to procure. Newbies might want to start with these.

Collectors are usually happy enough to own single stamps of each example. Investors, on the other hand, will look for errors and varieties, which usually increase the value of the stamps five to ten times (or even more). If you are looking for uncommon pieces, pay attention to the following details:

- Imperforation between vertical pairs
- Imperforation between horizontal pairs
- Surcharge inverted
- Surcharge double (sometimes one is inverted)
- Surcharge omitted
- Surcharge with spelling error
- Surcharge in an uncommon color
- Unusual paper, or unusual color

Another piece of high value Imperial Chinese stamps is the express letter stamps, the one below...

Depending on its condition, this type of stamps might realize up to $10,000 in auctions. The stamp was printed in booklet, in which different portions served different purposes. The left part was kept for control (audit) purposes. The other parts were issued to the addressee as receipt, or kept by the postman, or returned to the post office.

::: Foreign Post Offices in China :::

In general, stamps issued by Foreign Post Offices in China are not very expensive. Collectors, especially new collectors, might also consider venturing into this interesting area if they haven't done so.

The most costly examples observed include:

- United States Postal Agency Franklin stamps, up to a few hundreds of dollars in value

- Japan Post Offices: Those Yen values are mostly very rare and expensive. The most expensive is the 10y example depicting Princess Jingu, over $10,000. Besides, military stamps ("軍事") are extremely costly.

- Russian Post Offices: Issues of 1920 top the price list at three-digit catalogue values

- Italian Post Offices: So far the most expensive of all Foreign Post Offices issues. The most valuable types are the "Pechino 20c on 50c", "Pechino 40c on 1 Lire", "2 Dolari Pechino" on 5 Lire, worth five to six digits

- German Post Offices: The most expensive series is the diagonal overprint "China" on Germania stamps. The 50 pfennig below is worth five digits:

- French Post Offices: Postage Due (A Persevoir) are the most expensive. Below is one of those five-digit examples:

Similarly, errors and varieties will always cost an arm and a leg.

It makes more sense to also collect the main issues of the countries that have post offices in China, and their other colony issues, since they mostly bear the same designs. With this, you will start building up a solid specialization with China (Foreign Post Offices) being a subset of your specialization.

::: Formosa :::

Formosa has produced quite a number of valuable philatelic materials during this period.

The first postage stamps used in Taiwan was the overprint issues on 1886 Imperial China dragon stamps, on 3 candarins and 5 candarins values. Overprints show "Formosa" or "臺灣郵票" (Stamp of Taiwan). Both perforated and imperforated examples were produced. These stamps usually fetch thousands of dollars if listed in auctions.

The first official issue of Taiwan is the woodblock printing postage label as shown below. The right portion of the stamp was usually detached and used on the mail. The left portion was retained for control purposes. The stamps were imperforated.

The "Horse and Dragon" stamps were issued in 1888. Two values were issued as shown below.

Various hand-stamp patterns were used on these two stamps, showing the departure and destination of the mails. The following overprints were observed:

- "台北至錫口洋": Taipei to Yikou Foreign
- "水轉脚至錫口洋": Shuizhuanjiao to Yikou Foreign
- "台北至水轉脚洋": Taipei to Shuizhuanjiao Foreign
- "錫口": Yikou
- "水返脚": Shuifanjiao

Last but not least, the 1895 issues of Republic of Formosa exist in 3 Dies. Die I was issued imperforated. Die II and III were perforated.

::: Hong Kong :::

It makes more sense to collect earlier Hong Kong stamps if you are also a collector of British Commonwealth stamps. Most of the stamps would follow the Commonwealth designs or be a part of an Omnibus series.

This section goes a little bit out of the 1912 timeframe that we are investigating in Part A of the chapter.

I would like to highlight the following areas if you look into early Hong Kong philately:

Queen Victoria – QV (issues from 1862 to 1900): Various issues and surcharge. Stamps can be unwatermarked, or with watermark "Crown CC" or "Crown CA" shown below.

King Edward VII – KEVII (issues from 1903 to 1911): Three issues, printed on watermarked papers. 2 types of watermarks include "Crown CA" or "Multiple Crown CA".

King George V - KGV (issues from 1912 to 1937): Two issues, printed on watermarked papers. 2 types of watermarks include "Multiple Crown CA" or "Multiple Script CA".

King George VI – KGVI (issues from 1938 to 1952): Only one issue printed on "Multiple Script CA" watermarked papers.

You can also collect the following Omnibus issues of Hong Kong:

1935 Silver Jubilee of KGV: Complete set of 4 stamps, currently listed at £65 (MNH) or £18 (used) by Stanley Gibbons. Various varieties exist. This is part of the Commonwealth Silver Jubilee Omnibus series of 250 stamps, priced at £1,400 (unused) or £2,000 (used).

1937 Coronation of KGVI: Complete set of 3 stamps, currently listed at £25 (MNH) or £14 (used) by Stanley Gibbons. It is part of the Commonwealth 1937 Coronation Omnibus series of 202 stamps, priced at £200 (unused) or £250 (used).

1946 Victory issue: Complete set of 2 stamps, currently listed at £7 (MNH) or £3 (used) by Stanley Gibbons. It is part of the Commonwealth Victory Omnibus series of 164 stamps, priced at £55 (unused) or £90 (used). Hong Kong did not adopt the common design.

1948 Silver Wedding of KGVI: Complete set of 2 stamps, currently listed at £325 (MNH) or £130 (used) by Stanley Gibbons. It is part of the Commonwealth Silver Wedding Omnibus series of 138 stamps, priced at £2,250 (unused) or £2,500 (used).

1949 UPU issue: Complete set of 4 stamps, currently listed at £65 (MNH) or £18 (used) by Stanley Gibbons. It is part of the UPU Omnibus series of 310 stamps, priced at £325 (unused) or £600 (used).

1953 Coronation of Queen Elizabeth II – QEII: Only one stamp, currently listed at £3.5 (MNH) or 30 pence (used) by Stanley Gibbons. It is a part of the 1953 Coronation Omnibus series of 106 stamps, priced at £140 (unused) or £110 (used).

You can also consider collecting the "Specimen" examples of the abovementioned issues, which cost much more.

::: Macau :::

Again, it makes more sense to collect Macau as a sub-specialization of the "Portuguese and Colonies" stamp collection.

Used stamps are more affordable to collect. Below are a few expensive examples of early Macau philately:

| King Luis | King Carlos | Portuguese Republic |

If you want to venture into this specialization, get a Macau Catalogue. See Chapter 5 for more information.

B. Republic of China Period (1912 – 1949)

As a starting point, collectors can start with Sun Yat-sen & Martyrs definitive issues (including surcharge), the Junk definitive and the later commemorative issues, which are quite affordable and easy to complete. The further you go, the wider your scope of collection can be expanded. Below are those options for more advanced collectors.

::: Beiyang Government :::

For those who are collecting the Provisional surcharge issues of 1912, surcharge with "臨時中立" (Provisional Neutrality) is much more costly than those with "中華民國" (Republic of China) alone, especially those on the bean goose dollar values. Some of these stamps are currently listed at up to $10,000 in the catalogues.

The first two commemorative issues of the Republic of China in 1912 depicted Sun Yat-sen and Yuan Shikai. A complete mint set of both issues are listed over $1,000. Price of the used set is usually half of mint.

Each set has twelve stamps, with denomination ranging from one cent to $5.

The Sun Yat-sen set was issued to commemorate the Revolution, while the Yuan Shikai set was issued to celebrate the foundation of the Republic.

Facts & Figures: Sun Yat-sen & Yuan Shikai

Sun Yat-sen (孫逸仙, 1866 – 1925) is a Chinese revolutionary and founder of the Republic of China. He is one of the leaders of the Xinhai Revolution, overthrowing the Qing dynasty in 1912. He is also the co-founder of the Chinese Kuomintang (KMT).

His famous political philosophy is known as the Three Principles of the People (三民主义): nationalism, democracy, and the people's livelihood.

Yuan Shikai (袁世凯, 1859 – 1916) is a Chinese general, the first President of the Republic of China, and a self-acclaimed Emperor. He faced such widespread opposition that he had to abandon his monarchy in 1915 and died a year after that due to uremia.

Another well-sought-after set is the 1928 issue depicting Marshall Zhang Zuolin. The stamps were only valid in Hebei (back then known as Zhili) and Shandong. The issue was withdrawn when Chiang Kai-Shek unified China and established the new Nationalist Government.

Overprint exists for Xinjiang: "新疆贴用", Jilin and Heilongjiang: "吉黑贴用".

Facts & Figures: Zhang Zuolin

Zhang Zuolin (张作霖, 1875 – 1928) is the Marshall and a warlord of Manchuria during the Beiyang era of the Republic of China. He gained controlled of the Inner China and Manchuria in 1924 but was defeated by Chiang Kai-shek in 1928.

::: Nationalist Government :::

The first commemorative issue being produced after Chiang Kai-shek took control over China is the unification issue (1928). Overprints exist for Xinjiang: "新疆貼用", Yunnan: "滇省貼用", Jilin & Heilongjiang: "吉黑貼用".

Facts & Figures: Chiang Kai-shek

Chiang Kai-shek (蔣介石, 1887 – 1975) is the leader of the Republic of China from 1928 to 1975. He took over the leadership of Kuomintang after Sun Yat-sen's death. After being defeated by the Chinese Communist Party in 1949, his government and army retreated to Taiwan, where he led the Country and the Party until his death.

The Sun Yat-sen Mausoleum issue of 1929 is another set to pay attention to. Similar to the earlier Zhang Zuolin and Chiang Kai-shek issues, and also the later Tan Yankai issue, the $1 value is the most difficult to come by. Overprints exist for Xinjiang: "新疆貼用", Yunnan: "滇省貼用" and Jilin & Heilongjiang: "吉黑貼用".

Northwest Scientific Expedition commemorative issue of 1932 was printed to finance the expedition of Dr. Sven Hedin (1865 – 1952). The market price of this set is comparatively high compared to the previous few sets introduced.

Tan Yankai issue of 1933 is one of those few China stamps that show no country inscription on the design. Overprints also exist for this issue, with "新疆貼用" (Restricted for use in Xinjiang), and "滇省貼用" (Restricted for use in Yunnan).

The flying geese issue of 1949 is another high value set to collect. There are 4 official values: $1, $2, $5 and $10, and unissued values: 10c, 16c, 50c, $20 and $50. The 50c, $20 and $50 examples might cost three digits if come across in any auctions or listed for sale by any experienced collectors in the market.

Collectors who would like to specialize in surcharge stamps will need to study the catalogues very carefully and decide how to collect and categorize their stamps. So far, "國幣" (Chinese Nationalist Currency) and "金圓" (Gold Yuan) surcharges do not pose any difficulties for collectors to complete, except that there are too many of them, usually leading to confusion.

The best catalogues for this period are Chan Catalogue 2010 edition and China Stamp Society's 2016 Catalogue. Please refer to Chapter 5 of this book for more details.

The most expensive surcharge issue of this period is the 1942 "國內平信，附加已付" surcharge (Additional Charge for Domestic Normal Postage). 14 different overprints were used for 14 provinces. Below are a few examples:

Province surcharge during the war against Japan is another interesting area to study. Some of the surcharge types are quite valuable, especially those made in Guangdong province.

Out of 6 Airmail issues, the 1921 and 1929 issues are the most interesting. The only difference in the design of these two issues is the tail of the airplane, bearing the Beiyang emblem in the 1921 issue, while showing the Nationalist badge in the 1929 issue. The former cost at least three times of the latter.

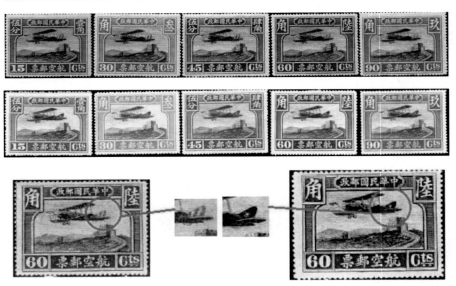

::: Japanese Occupation & Manchukuo :::

Japanese occupation surcharge is an area that needs a lot of time to study, since there are too many different overprint patterns for different occupied districts.

Manchukuo stamps are currently still affordable and easy to complete. The most valuable stamps are those with the portrait of Emperor Kangde (Puyi), especially the 15c with "Machuria State" inscription.

Facts & Figures: The Last Emperor of China

Asin-Gioro Puyi (溥仪, 1906 – 1967) is the last Emperor of China, also known as Emperor Xuan Tong, also the only Emperor of the Manchuria Empire (Manchukuo), known as Emperor Kang De. After the People's Republic of China was established in 1949, he lived in Beijing as a normal citizen.

::: Communist & Liberated Area :::

Due to the complexity of this specialization, we will focus more on the rare and special issues during this period. If you are interested in this specialization, look for the Yang Catalogue as a reference. I'll talk about that in Chapter 5.

All of the Red Post issues (1930 – 1932) and the Chinese Soviet Republic issues (1931 – 1936) are rare. Many of them are valued at five digits.

Below are the issues known to be produced or survived:

Southwest Jiangxi Red Post

Northeast Jiangxi Red Post

West Fujian Red Post

Jiangxi Red Post: This stamp (left) fetched $415,000 in InterAsia auction in 2014, since it is the only one known to survive.

West Hunan-Hubei Red Post (above right)

Hunan-Jiangxi Red Post

Chinese Soviet Republic: Below are a few major designs issued during this period. There are also different re-drawn types and varieties.

Common issues of the Liberated Areas are not rare and can be acquired easily these days.

Many of the issues depicted Mao Zedong and Zhu De. This can be made into a topic if someone wants to narrow down the scope of his collection.

Below are a few examples from many Mao Zedong issues during this period of time.

Central Plains

Shandong

Bohai

Jiangsu-Anhui

East China People's Post

North Anhui   *Shanxi-Chahar-Hebei Border*   *Hebei-Shandong-Henan Border*

Shanxi-Hebei-Shandong-Henan Border Area   *North China*   *Liaoning*

Andong

Northeast China People's Post

Northwest China People's Post

Facts & Figures: Mao Zedong & Zhu De

Mao Zedong (Mao Tse Tung, 毛泽东, 1893 – 1976) is the founding father of the People's Republic of China. He is also one of the founding members of the Chinese Communist Party and the Red Army. He is regarded as one of the most important figures in Modern History.

Zhu De (Chu Teh, 朱德, 1886 – 1976) is a Chinese general, politician and revolutionary. He is one of the pioneers of the Chinese Communist Party. He is regarded as the principal founder of the People's Liberation Army and is one of the ten Marshals of the forces.

Stamps depicting Zhu De are much fewer in quantity. Below are a few examples:

Again, Liberated Area is a complex specialization. If you are into this area, I suggest you study the Yang Catalogue for further information since the scope of this book cannot go into much details. That can make a separate book itself.

Stanley Gibbons is another good catalogue that you can refer to since it covers almost everything related to this topic.

C. People's Republic of China, Hong Kong, Macau and Taiwan after 1949

This part covers various highly demanded sets of China stamps from 1949 onwards. We'll cover all Mainland China (PRC), Hong Kong, Macau & Taiwan.

For PRC issues, we'll look at the moving average of 5-year value estimation in key markets, including East Asia (China, Hong Kong, Macau, Taiwan, Japan and Korea), North America (US & Canada), Europe and Southeast Asia (Singapore as the representative). The estimation is made based on expert advice (through latest catalogues) and commercial price in shops, auctions and private treaty sales. The numbers illustrated herein are not exactly the same as any catalogues or commercial price tags, but they represent the common value that you might come across in each market. Average market value will be derived in USD. As a reference, you can look at it as the fair value to avoid overpaying in any of your purchase and underselling in any of your sale or consignment.

I'll also illustrate the average market value of the previous 20 years so that you can see the trend and make a comparison. Similarly, these numbers are also derived from different catalogues during the 1995/2000 period.

::: PRC C-Headed Issues :::

There are North East issues for C1 to C8, using different currency. Reprint exists for issues from C1 to C13 (including C1NE to C8NE). The value difference between the reprints and original stamps are quite substantial. This section examines the basic price difference, along with major design differences between the original and the reprint issue. If you have a chance to invest in the first few C-headed issues, go for the original ones, as much as possible.

C1 & C1NE – First Session of Chinese People's Consultative Political Conference
Date of issue: 8 Oct, 1949 | Date of reprint: 10 Jan, 1955

	Mint		Used	
	Original	**Reprint**	**Original**	**Reprint**
Europe	€34	€10	€20	€2
North America	$45	$15	$20	$3
East Asia	¥250	¥100	¥150	¥30
Southeast Asia	$35	$12	$18	$6
Average 2015/20	**$40**	**$15**	**$25**	**$4**
Average 1995/00	**$10**	**$2**	**$10**	**$1**

While using the same design as the general issues, there's an inscription on the stamps to illustrate the North East issues.

	Mint		Used	
	Original	Reprint	Original	Reprint
Europe	€220	€10	€250	€6
North America	$180	$15	$45	$12
East Asia	¥2,000	¥100	¥1,200	¥60
Southeast Asia	$220	$12	$140	$7
Average 2015/20	**$260**	**$15**	**$180**	**$9**
Average 1995/00	**$18**	**$2**	**$20**	**$1**

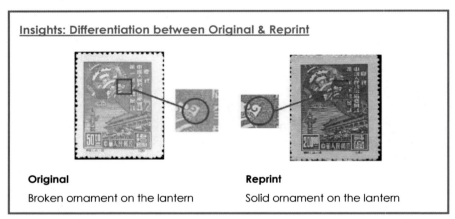

Insights: Differentiation between Original & Reprint

Original

Broken ornament on the lantern

Reprint

Solid ornament on the lantern

C2 & C2NE – Chinese People's Consultative Political Conference
Date of issue: 1 Feb, 1950 | Date of reprint: 10 Jan, 1955

	Mint		Used	
	Original	**Reprint**	**Original**	**Reprint**
Europe	€45	€12	€30	€3
North America	$45	$20	$40	$7
East Asia	¥350	¥120	¥250	¥70
Southeast Asia	$55	$14	$30	$8
Average 2015/20	**$60**	**$18**	**$40**	**$8**
Average 1995/00	**$12**	**$4**	**$15**	**$3**

	Mint		Used	
	Original	**Reprint**	**Original**	**Reprint**
Europe	€200	€15	€250	€7
North America	$150	$12	$140	$12
East Asia	¥1,800	¥120	¥2,000	¥70
Southeast Asia	$260	$14	$280	$9
Average 2015/20	**$250**	**$17**	**$280**	**$11**
Average 1995/00	**$45**	**$5**	**$50**	**$3**

Insights: Differentiation between Original & Reprint

On (4-1) and (4-2)

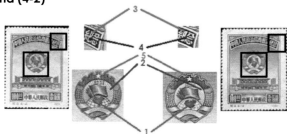

	Original	**Reprint**
1	Globe lines and China map are clearly defined	Designs of globe lines and China map are less sharp
2	Background lines touch the upper edge of the emblem	Background lines don't touch the upper edge of the emblem
3	Character "紀": Larger space in "巳"	Character "紀": Smaller space in "巳"
4	Character "念": First stroke (╱) touches third stroke (–)	Character "念": Second stroke (╲) touches third stroke (–)
5	Shorter star	Taller star

On (4-3) and (4-4)

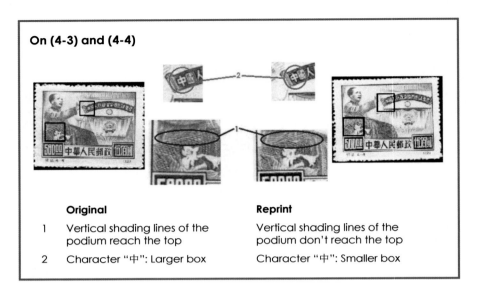

	Original	Reprint
1	Vertical shading lines of the podium reach the top	Vertical shading lines of the podium don't reach the top
2	Character "中": Larger box	Character "中": Smaller box

C3 & C3NE – World Federation of Trade Union Congress
Date of issue: 16 Nov, 1949 | Date of reprint: 10 Jan, 1955

	Mint		Used	
	Original	Reprint	Original	Reprint
Europe	€50	€4	€35	€3
North America	$70	$8	$20	$3
East Asia	¥400	¥60	¥280	¥35
Southeast Asia	$70	$8	$35	$4
Average 2015/20	**$70**	**$8**	**$38**	**$4**
Average 1995/00	**$20**	**$3**	**$15**	**$2**

	Mint		Used	
	Original	**Reprint**	**Original**	**Reprint**
Europe	€4,000	€300	€1,000	€120
North America	$2,500	$550	$800	$450
East Asia	¥40,000	¥2,300	¥15,000	¥1,500
Southeast Asia	$5,800	$320	$1,600	$300
Average 2015/20	**$5,200**	**$425**	**$1,600**	**$300**
Average 1995/00	**$350**	**$120**	**$200**	**$60**

Insights: Differentiation between Original & Reprint

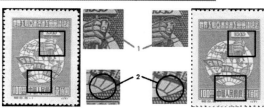

	Original	**Reprint**
1	Fingers are lightly shaded	Fingers are heavily shaded
2	2nd longitude doesn't touch the hemisphere	2nd longitude touches the hemisphere

C4 & C4NE – Inauguration of the People's Republic
Date of issue: 1 Jul, 1950 | Date of reprint: 10 Jan, 1955

	Mint		Used	
	Original	**Reprint**	**Original**	**Reprint**
Europe	€400	€15	€60	€3
North America	$400	$40	$100	$15
East Asia	¥3,000.00	¥250.00	¥800	¥150
Southeast Asia	$720	$38	$350	$25
Average 2015/20	**$550**	**$35**	**$170**	**$17**
Average 1995/00	**$120**	**$6**	**$50**	**$3**

	Mint		Used	
	Original	**Reprint**	**Original**	**Reprint**
Europe	€1,200	€35	€1,000	€15
North America	$1,000	$50	$450	$45
East Asia	¥12,000	¥260	¥7,000	¥200
Southeast Asia	$1,800	$38	$500	$30
Average 2015/20	**$1,600**	**$45**	**$900**	**$30**
Average 1995/00	**$250**	**$6**	**$220**	**$3**

Insights: Differentiation between Original & Reprints

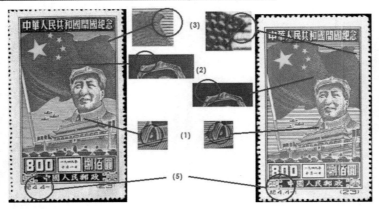

	Original	**Reprint**
1	Half circle arc in Mao Zedong's shirt button	A little dot in Mao Zedong's shirt button
2	More shading dots in the area above Mao Zedong's cap	Fewer shading dots in the area above Mao Zedong's cap
3	Shading lines don't touch the flag	Shading lines touch the flag
4	Perforation: P14	Perforation: P12½
5	"." after "紀4" is not clear	Bold and clear "." after "紀4"

C6 & C6NE – First Anniversary of the People's Republic
Date of issue: 1 Oct, 1950 and 30 Oct, 1950
Date of reprint: 10 Jan, 1955

	Mint		Used	
	Original	**Reprint**	**Original**	**Reprint**
Europe	€250	€15	€70	€3
North America	$300	$20	$100	$10
East Asia	¥2,000	¥120	¥1,200	¥70
Southeast Asia	$300	$20	$240	$10
Average 2015/20	**$330**	**$20**	**$160**	**$9**
Average 1995/00	**$120**	**$4**	**$50**	**$3**

	Mint		Used	
	Original	**Reprint**	**Original**	**Reprint**
Europe	€1,200	€25	€1,000	€10
North America	$1,000	$40	$250	$35
East Asia	¥12,000	¥140	¥10,000	¥100
Southeast Asia	$1,700	$20	$1,500	$18
Average 2015/20	**$1,600**	**$30**	**$1,200**	**$20**
Average 1995/00	**$300**	**$4**	**$250**	**$3**

Insights: Differentiation between Original & Reprint

On (5-3)

	Original	**Reprint**
1	Shading dots form 45-degree angle	Shading dots form 72-degree angle
2	Darker red flag	Brighter red flag
3	"." after "紀6" is not clear	Clearer "." after "紀6"

On (5-1), (5-2), (5-4) and (5-5)

	Original	**Reprint**
1	Reddish-brown leaves, fully-shaded	Grey-brown leaves, with a white part in between
2	Flag ribbon is less curvy and there's a flat (straight) parts at the base	Flag ribbon is more curvy compared to the original
3	"." after "紀6" is not clear	Clearer "." after "紀6"

C7 & C7NE – First All-China Postal Conference
Date of issue: 1 Nov, 1950 | Date of reprint: 10 Jan, 1955

	Mint		Used	
	Original	**Reprint**	**Original**	**Reprint**
Europe	€80	€2	€12	€2
North America	$70	$3	$20	$2
East Asia	¥500	¥20	¥300	¥15
Southeast Asia	$60	$2	$40	$2
Average 2015/20	**$85**	**$3**	**$30**	**$3**
Average 1995/00	**$10**	**$2**	**$6**	**$1**

	Mint		Used	
	Original	**Reprint**	**Original**	**Reprint**
Europe	€80	€4	€75	€2
North America	$80	$5	$40	$3
East Asia	¥700	¥25	¥400	¥15
Southeast Asia	$120	$2.5	$80	$2
Average 2015/20	**$100**	**$4**	**$75**	**$3**
Average 1995/00	**$12**	**$2**	**$12**	**$1**

<u>Insights: Differentiation between Original & Reprint</u>

Original

1 Three lines under character "一"

2 Perforation: P14

Reprint

Four lines under character "一"

Perforation: P12½

C8 & C8NE – Sino-Soviet Treaty
Date of issue: 1 Dec, 1950 | Date of reprint: 10 Jan, 1955

	Mint		Used	
	Original	**Reprint**	**Original**	**Reprint**
Europe	€75	€15	€20	€2
North America	$70	$15	$30	$7
East Asia	¥650	¥120	¥400	¥50
Southeast Asia	$100	$15	$80	$8
Average 2015/20	**$100**	**$18**	**$50**	**$7**
Average 1995/00	**$40**	**$5**	**$20**	**$3**

	Mint		Used	
	Original	**Reprint**	**Original**	**Reprint**
Europe	€80	€15	€60	€3
North America	$80	$15	$50	$10
East Asia	¥500	¥130	¥350	¥60
Southeast Asia	$80	$18	$100	$12
Average 2015/20	**$90**	**$20**	**$75**	**$9**
Average 1995/00	**$40**	**$5**	**$45**	**$3**

Insights: Differentiation between Original & Reprint

	Original	**Reprint**
1	(3-2) is deep green	(3-2) is yellow green
2	The background map is more heavily shaded	The background map is less shaded compared to original

C9 – 30th Anniversary of the Chinese Communist Party
Date of issue: 1 Jul, 1951 | Date of reprint: 10 Jan, 1955

	Mint		Used	
	Original	Reprint	Original	Reprint
Europe	€30	€14	€15	€3
North America	$35	$20	$18	$12
East Asia	¥350	¥150	¥180	¥70
Southeast Asia	$55	$20	$25	$10
Average 2015/20	**$48**	**$20**	**$23**	**$9**
Average 1995/00	**$20**	**$4**	**$10**	**$2**

Insights: Differentiation between Original & Reprint

	Original	Reprint
1	Thicker paper	Whiter and thinner paper
2	Background heavily shaded	Background lightly shaded. Dots can be seen more clearly

---

C10 – World Peace Campaign (2nd Issue)
Date of issue: 15 Aug, 1951 | Date of reprint: 10 Jan, 1955

	Mint		Used	
	Original	Reprint	Original	Reprint
Europe	€50	€20	€15	€2
North America	$70	$30	$35	$8
East Asia	¥550	¥200	¥300	¥50
Southeast Asia	$110	$34	$70	$14
Average 2015/20	**$85**	**$30**	**$45**	**$8**
Average 1995/00	**$30**	**$12**	**$15**	**$6**

Imperforation between pairs yield very high value.

Insights: Differentiation between Original & Reprint

	Original	Reprint
1	Perforation: P14	Perforation: P12½
2	On (3-1) & (3-3): A dotted half circle at the button	A star at the button
3	On (3-2) & (3-3): A line on the leave	"X" shape on the leave

C11 – 15th Death Anniversary of Lu Xun
Date of issue: 19 Oct, 1951 | Date of reprint: 10 Jan, 1955

	Mint		Used	
	Original	Reprint	Original	Reprint
Europe	€30	€3	€8	€1
North America	$25	$5	$10	$2
East Asia	¥250	¥30	¥150	¥18
Southeast Asia	$40	$4	$25	$2
Average 2015/20	**$38**	**$5**	**$18**	**$2**
Average 1995/00	**$10**	**$1**	**$4**	**$0.5**

Insights: Differentiation between Original & Reprint

Original	Reprint
No dot in the lower right corner	A little dot in the lower right corner

Facts & Figures: Lu Xun

Lu Xun (Lu Hsun – 鲁迅), Zhou Shuren by birth, (1881 – 1936) is a leading figure of modern Chinese literature. His exerted a substantial influence on Chinese literature and popular culture during his time. He was highly acclaimed by the Chinese government after the PRC was founded. Mao Zedong himself was a lifelong admirer of Lu Xun's works.

C12 – Centenary of Taiping Rebellion
Date of issue: 15 Dec, 1951 | Date of reprint: 10 Jan, 1955

	Mint		Used	
	Original	Reprint	Original	Reprint
Europe	€70	€3	€20	€1
North America	$65	$8	$25	$3
East Asia	¥450	¥45	¥350	¥30
Southeast Asia	$58	$5	$50	$3
Average 2015/20	**$75**	**$6**	**$40**	**$3**
Average 1995/00	**$25**	**$3**	**$15**	**$1**

Insights: Differentiation between Original & Reprint

On (4-1) and (4-3)

Original

Top left corner shading is clear

Reprint

There are 2 extra lines at the top left corner

On (4-2) and (4-4)

Original

Normal design

Reprint

There are 2 extra strokes on a bottom right parts of the coin

---

Facts & Figures: The Taiping Rebellion

The Taiping Rebellion is a civil war in China, starting in 1850, between the Qing dynasty and the Christian millenarian movement of the Heavenly Kingdom of Peace (Taiping Tianguo). This movement was led by Hong Xiuquan.

The Taiping troop was finally defeated in 1864. Over 50 million people were estimated to die during this massive war.

C13 – Liberation of Tibet
Date of issue: 15 Mar, 1952 | Date of reprint: 10 Jan, 1955

	Mint		Used	
	Original	**Reprint**	**Original**	**Reprint**
Europe	€70	€12	€20	€2
North America	$60	$20	$25	$6
East Asia	¥450	¥120	¥250	¥70
Southeast Asia	$70	$15	$40	$7
Average 2015/20	**$78**	**$18**	**$35**	**$7**
Average 1995/00	**$25**	**$3**	**$12**	**$1**

Insights: Differentiation between Original & Reprints

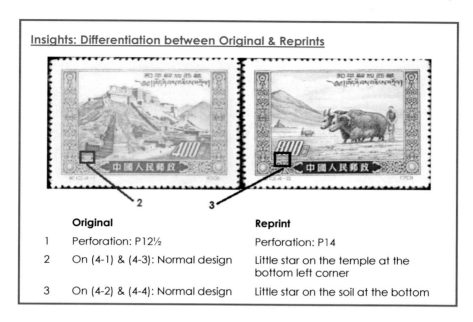

	Original	Reprint
1	Perforation: P12½	Perforation: P14
2	On (4-1) & (4-3): Normal design	Little star on the temple at the bottom left corner
3	On (4-2) & (4-4): Normal design	Little star on the soil at the bottom

C20 – 35th Anniversary of the Russian Revolution
Date of issue: 5 Oct, 1953

	Mint	Used
Europe	€5	€2
North America	$12	$4
East Asia	¥55	¥25
Southeast Asia	$7	$4
Average 2015/20	**$9**	**$4**
Average 1995/00	**$3**	**$1.5**

Insights: Rarities

The set that we usually see in the market shows the inscription "偉大的十月革命三十五週年紀念" (35th anniversary of the Great October Revolution). This set is not expensive.

There is another version of this issue, bearing the same design, with different colors and two additional Chinese characters in the inscription: "偉大的蘇聯十月革命三十五週年紀念" (35th anniversary of the <u>Soviet</u> Great October Revolution).

The stamps were unofficially released in several post offices and withdrawn shortly after that. Only a small number was sold to the market. The current value of this set is over $45,000 (mint) or $20,000 (used).

Facts & Figures: The Russian October Revolution

There were two revolutions in Russia in 1917: The February Revolution, overthrowing the imperial government of the Tsar; and the October Revolution, placing the Bolsheviks in power.

The October Revolution took place on 7th November 1917 (or 25th October, based on Old Style (Julian) calendar), with an armed insurrection in Petrograd.

Consequences

- Establishment of the Soviet Russia
- End of Russian Provisional Government, Russian Republic and dual power
- Start of the Russian Civil War

C33 & C33M – Ancient Chinese Scientists (1st Issue)
Date of issue: 25 Aug, 1955

	Mint	Used
Europe	€20	€2
North America	$25	$4
East Asia	¥150	¥25
Southeast Asia	$20	$3
Average 2015/20	**$25**	**$4**
Average 1995/00	**$8**	**$2**

	Mint	Used
Europe	€200	€90
North America	$250	$70
East Asia	¥1,600	¥400
Southeast Asia	$250	$72
Average 2015/20	**$270**	**$85**
Average 1995/00	**$60**	**$18**

C34 – 85th Birth Anniversary of Lenin
Date of issue: 15 Dec, 1955

	Mint	Used
Europe	€45	€3
North America	$38	$3
East Asia	¥280	¥30
Southeast Asia	$45	$4.5
Average 2015/20	**$50**	**$4**
Average 1995/00	**$12**	**$2**

C35 – 135th Birth Anniversary of Engels
Date of issue: 15 Dec, 1955

	Mint	Used
Europe	€45	€3
North America	$38	$3
East Asia	¥280	¥30
Southeast Asia	$45	$4.5
Average 2015/20	**$50**	**$4**
Average 1995/00	**$12**	**$2**

Facts & Figures: Freidrich Engels & V.I. Lenin

Engels (1820 – 1895) is a German philosopher, social scientist and journalist. He is the co-founder of Marxist theory, together with Karl Marx. In 1848 he and Marx published The Communist Manifesto; And later he supported Marx in his famous works Das Kapital.

Lenin (1870 – 1924), Vladimir Ilyich Ulyanov by birth, is a Russian politician and revolutionary, well-known to be the founder of the very first Communist state in the world, after the success of the Russian October Revolution. His political theories are known as Leninism.

C38 – 90ᵗʰ Birth Anniversary of Sun Yat-sen
Date of issue: 12 Nov, 1956

	Mint	Used
Europe	€40	€4
North America	$45	$6
East Asia	¥320	¥30
Southeast Asia	$50	$4
Average 2015/20	**$50**	**$5**
Average 1995/00	**$15**	**$2**

C41 – 30ᵗʰ Anniversary of the People's Liberation Army
Date of issue: 1957

	Mint	Used
Europe	€100	€4
North America	$120	$10
East Asia	¥750	¥60
Southeast Asia	$110	$6
Average 2015/20	**$130**	**$8**
Average 1995/00	**$30**	**$3**

C44 – 40ᵗʰ Anniversary of Russian Revolution
Date of issue: 7 Nov, 1957

	Mint	Used
Europe	€70	€2
North America	$65	$5
East Asia	¥420	¥40
Southeast Asia	$55	$8
Average 2015/20	**$75**	**$6**
Average 1995/00	**$30**	**$3**

C46 – 140ᵗʰ Birth Anniversary of Karl Marx
Date of issue: 5 May, 1958

	Mint	Used
Europe	€50	€4
North America	$40	$5
East Asia	¥300	¥40
Southeast Asia	$45	$5
Average 2015/20	**$50**	**$6**
Average 1995/00	**$15**	**$3**

Facts & Figures: Karl Marx

Karl Marx (1818 – 1883) is a German philosopher, journalist, economist, sociologist and the founder of Marxism. He is recognized as one of the most influential figures in human history. Two of his most notable works are The Communist Manifesto and Das Kapital.

Insights: Related Issue

There are quite a few issues featuring Karl Marx, Freiderich Engels and Lenin that you can look out for.
- Marx: C22 (1953), C46 (1958), C98 (1963), J90 (1983)
- Engels: C35 (1955) & C80 (1960)
- Lenin: C26 (1954), C34 (1955), C77 (1960), C111 (1965), J57 (1980)

C47 & C47M – Unveiling of People's Heroes Monument
Date of issue: 1 May, 1958

Stamp	Mint	Used
Europe	€45	€3
North America	$40	$4
East Asia	¥280	¥25
Southeast Asia	$38	$4
Average 2015/20	**$50**	**$4**
Average 1995/00	**$12**	**$2**

Miniature Sheet	Mint	Used
Europe	€200	€100
North America	$250	$80
East Asia	¥2,500	¥600
Southeast Asia	$330	$90
Average 2015/20	**$320**	**$100**
Average 1995/00	**$75**	**$40**

C50 & C50M – 700th Anniversary of Guan Hanqing's Works
Date of issue: 20 Jun, 1958

Stamps	Mint	Used
Europe	€80	€4
North America	$90	$10
East Asia	¥650	¥50
Southeast Asia	$110	$10
Average 2015/20	**$110**	**$9**
Average 1995/00	**$25**	**$5**

Miniature Sheet	Mint	Used
Europe	€350	€120
North America	$500	$150
East Asia	¥3,000	¥800
Southeast Asia	$550	$130
Average 2015/20	**$520**	**$150**
Average 1995/00	**$120**	**$60**

Facts & Figures: Guan Hanqing

Guan Hanqing (Kuan Han Ching – 关汉卿, circa 1241 – 1320), is a prolific Chinese playwright and poet, living during the Yuan Dynasty. He is known to have produced more than 60 plays during his lifetime. Only 18 of those were preserved until today.

Insights: Related Issue

Collectors might also be interested to add the USSR's 1958 Guan Hanqing issue to their collection, as an accompaniment to their C50 issue!

Insights: Thematic

This issue can fit into various thematic collections. It can belong to the famous people collection. It can also be part of the Chinese opera & performing arts collection that we are going to mention in the next sections of the chapter.

C54 – 5th International Student's Union Congress
Date of issue: 4 Sep, 1958

	Mint	Used
Europe	€50	€2
North America	$55	$8
East Asia	¥380	¥30
Southeast Asia	$60	$3
Average 2015/20	**$65**	**$5**
Average 1995/00	**$15**	**$2**

Insights: Rarities

The original stamps were supposed to be issued on 1 Sep 1958, with the following inscription: "第五届世界学生代表大会" (5th World Student Representatives' Congress). However, before the official issuance, it was changed into "国际学联第五代表大会" (5th International Student's Union Congress). A small number of the former version was sold in advance and thus survived until today. Such a set will cost over $150,000 if ever being come across.

C58 – Great Leap Forward in Steel Production
Date of issue: 19 Feb & 25 May, 1959

	Mint	Used
Europe	€75	€4
North America	$100	$7
East Asia	¥750	¥30
Southeast Asia	$90	$4
Average 2015/20	**$110**	**$6**
Average 1995/00	**$12**	**$3**

Facts & Figures: The Great Leap Forward

Occurring between 1958 and 1961, the Great Leap Forward is Chinese Communist Party's economic and social campaign, with an objective to rapidly transform the country's economy through rapid industrialization and collectivization.

Major initiatives during the Great Leap Forward:

- People's Commune – issue S35 (1959)

- Industrialization and Steel Production – C58 (1959)

- Irrigation & Water Conservancy campaigns

- Agricultural Innovation – C60 (1959)

C62 – 40ᵗʰ Anniversary of the May 4ᵗʰ Movement
Date of issue: 1 Jul, 1959

	Mint	Used
Europe	€60	€15
North America	$80	$20
East Asia	¥600	¥150
Southeast Asia	$80	$22
Average 2015/20	**$90**	**$20**
Average 1995/00	**$25**	**$9**

Facts & Figures: The May Fourth Movement

The May Fourth Movement of 1919 is an anti-imperialist, cultural, and political movement in Beijing, especially protesting against the Beiyang government's weak response to the Shandong dispute with Japan after the World War I. This significant event marked a gain in popularity of Chinese Nationalism, and paving the way to the birth and development of Chinese Communism.

C67 – 10th Anniversary of the People's Republic (1st issue)
Date of issue: 28 Sep, 1959

	Mint	Used
Europe	€80	€10
North America	$100	$12
East Asia	¥1,200	¥90
Southeast Asia	$210	$13
Average 2015/20	**$160**	**$14**
Average 1995/00	**$25**	**$6**

C68 – 10th Anniversary of the People's Republic (2nd issue)
Date of issue: 1 Oct, 1959

	Mint	Used
Europe	€70	€10
North America	$80	$20
East Asia	¥500	¥70
Southeast Asia	$75	$12
Average 2015/20	**$85**	**$15**
Average 1995/00	**$25**	**$8**

C69 – 10th Anniversary of the People's Republic (3rd issue)
Date of issue: 1 Oct, 1959

	Mint	Used
Europe	€30	€3
North America	$40	$10
East Asia	¥350	¥60
Southeast Asia	$62	$12
Average 2015/20	**$50**	**$9**
Average 1995/00	**$10**	**$4**

C70 – 10th Anniversary of the People's Republic (4th issue)
Date of issue: 1 Oct, 1959

	Mint	Used
Europe	€40	€6
North America	$50	$7
East Asia	¥320	¥60
Southeast Asia	$48	$12
Average 2015/20	**$50**	**$9**
Average 1995/00	**$10**	**$4**

C71 – 10th Anniversary of the People's Republic (5th issue)
Date of issue: 1 Oct, 1959

	Mint	Used
Europe	€280	€45
North America	$250	$80
East Asia	¥1,800	¥500
Southeast Asia	$260	$70
Average 2015/20	**$300**	**$75**
Average 1995/00	**$25**	**$8**

C74 – 25th Anniversary of the Zunyi Conference during the Long March
Date of issue: 25 Jan, 1960

	Mint	Used
Europe	€150	€14
North America	$250	$30
East Asia	¥2,000	¥180
Southeast Asia	$300	$28
Average 2015/20	**$280**	**$27**
Average 1995/00	**$30**	**$8**

C75 – 10th Anniversary of Sino-Soviet Treaty
Date of issue: 10 Mar, 1960

	Mint	Used
Europe	€80	€14
North America	$100	$15
East Asia	¥900	¥100
Southeast Asia	$125	$22
Average 2015/20	**$125**	**$20**
Average 1995/00	**$20**	**$10**

C78 – 15th Anniversary of Hungarian Liberation
Date of issue: 4 Apr, 1960

	Mint	Used
Europe	€50	€10
North America	$100	$14
East Asia	¥800	¥70
Southeast Asia	$120	$12
Average 2015/20	**$110**	**$13**
Average 1995/00	**$15**	**$5**

C79 – 15th Anniversary of Liberation of Czechslovakia
Date of issue: 9 May, 1960

	Mint	Used
Europe	€50	€10
North America	$90	$14
East Asia	¥800	¥70
Southeast Asia	$120	$12
Average 2015/20	**$110**	**$13**
Average 1995/00	**$15**	**$5**

C81 – Third National Literary and Art Workers' Congress
Date of issue: 30 Jul, 1960

	Mint	Used
Europe	€60	€10
North America	$100	$14
East Asia	¥850	¥70
Southeast Asia	$110	$12
Average 2015/20	**$110**	**$13**
Average 1995/00	**$15**	**$4**

C82 – 15th Anniversary of North Korean Liberation
Date of issue: 15 Aug, 1960

	Mint	Used
Europe	€70	€15
North America	$120	$25
East Asia	¥950	¥180
Southeast Asia	$150	$24
Average 2015/20	**$130**	**$25**
Average 1995/00	**$25**	**$10**

C85 – 90th Anniversary of Paris Commune
Date of issue: 18 Mar, 1961

	Mint	Used
Europe	€50	€4
North America	$80	$25
East Asia	¥500	¥120
Southeast Asia	$78	$12
Average 2015/20	**$80**	**$16**
Average 1995/00	**$20**	**$5**

Facts & Figures: Paris Commune

The Paris Commune of 1871 is a radical socialist and revolutionary government ruling Paris from 18 March to 28 May, after France's defeat in the Franco-Prussian War and the collapse of the Second Empire. The new French government concluded the war with Prussia on harsh terms, paving the way for the Prussian occupation of Paris. In response to this, frustrated workers of Paris refused to cooperate with the Prussian soldiers, which subsequently led to an armed confrontation between the French government and the workers. Paris Commune was proclaimed as the government of the workers. In less than three months after the Commune was elected, 30,000 unarmed workers were massacred, thousands more were arrested and 7,000 were exiled by the French government. Despite being one of the most traumatic events in modern history, Paris Commune is considered as the first successful worker's revolution in the world.

C86M – 26th World Table Tennis Championship
Date of issue: 5 Apr, 1961

	Mint	Used
Europe	€1,000	€800
North America	$1,200	$1,000
East Asia	¥8,000	¥6,000
Southeast Asia	$1,250	$1,000
Average 2015/20	**$1,300**	**$1,000**
Average 1995/00	**$400**	**$250**

There's a variation of the sheet in which the golden decoration is omitted during printing. This may worth at least $20,000 (mint).

The stamp set itself doesn't worth that much. That's why we only look at the miniature sheet here. But the stamp set should be collected to accompany this miniature sheet.

C88 – 40th Anniversary of Chinese Communist Party
Date of issue: 1 Jul, 1961

	Mint	Used
Europe	€300	€15
North America	$400	$35
East Asia	¥4,500	¥250
Southeast Asia	$500	$45
Average 2015/20	**$520**	**$36**
Average 1995/00	**$60**	**$10**

C89 – 40th Anniversary of Mongolian People's Revolution
Date of issue: 11 Jul, 1961

	Mint	Used
Europe	€150	€30
North America	$280	$45
East Asia	¥2,100	¥280
Southeast Asia	$280	$45
Average 2015/20	**$280**	**$45**
Average 1995/00	**$20**	**$10**

C90 – 50th Anniversary of 1911 Revolution
Date of issue: 10 Oct, 1961

	Mint	Used
Europe	€90	€7
North America	$150	$7
East Asia	¥900	¥50
Southeast Asia	$130	$10
Average 2015/20	**$140**	**$9**
Average 1995/00	**$20**	**$5**

Facts & Figures: The Xinhai Revolution

The Xinhai Revolution (or Hsin Hai Revolution in old terms) overthrew the Qing dynasty and established the Republic of China on 1 January 1912. Many revolutionaries and groups during this period wanted to overthrow the Qing government. In 1905, Sun Yat-sen established the Tongmenghui (United League) that led about 10 uprisings, all of which failed until the Wuchang Uprising in October 1911. The revolution ended with the abdication of Emperor Puyi on 12 February 1912. The Revolution was supported by many groups, including students, intellectuals, overseas Chinese, soldiers and farmers etc.

C92 – Ancient Chinese Scientists (2nd Issue)
Date of issue: 1 Dec, 1962

	Mint	Used
Europe	€90	€10
North America	$120	$55
East Asia	¥800	¥250
Southeast Asia	$125	$25
Average 2015/20	**$130**	**$35**
Average 1995/00	**$35**	**$10**

Insights: Rarities

There's an error version on the (8-1) stamp – Cai Lun. Instead of showing his profile as "Cai Lun (? – 121)", the designer put "Cai Lun (BC? – 121)" by mistake (公元前). The stamp was stopped issuing after that. But a few thousand copies were not returned. Nowadays, a copy of such stamp will cost about $20,000 (mint) or $4,000 (used). Beware of counterfeit if you come across such stamp in the market!

C94 & C94M – Stage Arts of Mei Lanfang
Date of issue: 8 Aug, 1962

Perforated	Mint	Used
Europe	€1,500	€250
North America	$2,200	$320
East Asia	¥15,000	¥2,500
Southeast Asia	$2,800	$500
Average 2015/20	**$2,400**	**$400**
Average 1995/00	**$300**	**$100**

Imperforated	Mint	Used
Europe	€8,000	€5,000
North America	$8,500	$2,500
East Asia	¥60,000	¥20,000
Southeast Asia	$11,500	$3,000
Average 2015/20	**$10,000**	**$4,000**
Average 1995/00	**$2,500**	**$1,500**

M/S	Mint	Used
Europe	€15,000	€10,000
North America	$20,000	$8,000
East Asia	¥140,000	¥60,000
Southeast Asia	$20,000	$7,000
Average 2015/20	**$21,000**	**$10,000**
Average 1995/00	**$2,500**	**$1,000**

We'll revisit this set later in another section on thematic collection.

Facts & Figures: Mei Lanfang

Mei Lanfang (梅兰芳, 1894 – 1961) is one of the most famous Beijing opera artists of modern China. He made his stage debut at the age of 10. He is famous in playing female characters. He is the first artist to bring Beijing Opera out of China, during his world tour to North America and Europe, and had a chance to interact with various international artists of his time, including Charlie Chaplin, Douglas Fairbanks, Mary Pickford and Bertold Brecht.

Insights: Thematic

In addition to the Guan Hanqing issue that we saw earlier, C94 is a great set that you may try to possess. We'll revisit this set in the performing arts thematic section.

C95 – 45th Anniversary of the Russian Revolution
Date of issue: 7 Nov, 1962

	Mint	Used
Europe	€120	€7
North America	$250	$15
East Asia	¥2,300	¥100
Southeast Asia	$350	$20
Average 2015/20	**$290**	**$16**
Average 1995/00	**$30**	**$5**

C97 – 4th Anniversary of Cuban Revolution
Date of issue: 1 Jan, 1963

	Mint	Used
Europe	€500	€80
North America	$750	$120
East Asia	¥5,500	¥800
Southeast Asia	$900	$120
Average 2015/20	**$830**	**$125**
Average 1995/00	**$200**	**$30**

C102 – 5th Anniversary of Cuban Liberation
Date of issue: 1 Jan, 1964

	Mint	Used
Europe	€100	€15
North America	$120	$20
East Asia	¥850	¥90
Southeast Asia	$140	$12
Average 2015/20	**$140**	**$17**
Average 1995/00	**$20**	**$8**

C104 – Labor Day
Date of issue: 1 May, 1964

	Mint	Used
Europe	€90	€15
North America	$120	$15
East Asia	¥700	¥90
Southeast Asia	$110	$14
Average 2015/20	**$120**	**$17**
Average 1995/00	**$20**	**$8**

C106 & C106M – 15th Anniversary of the People's Repulic
Date of issue: 1 Oct, 1964

	Se-tenant strips		Separate stamps	
	Mint	**Used**	**Mint**	**Used**
Europe	€300	€30	€90	€10
North America	$300	$80	$100	$15
East Asia	¥4,000	¥400	¥1,000	¥120
Southeast Asia	$500	$60	$300	$25
Average 2015/20	**$480**	**$60**	**$175**	**$18**
Average 1995/00	**$100**	**$15**	**$50**	**$8**

Miniature Sheet	**Mint**	**Used**
Europe	€5,000	€2,000
North America	$4,000	$1,500
East Asia	¥30,000	¥12,000
Southeast Asia	$4,200	$1,500
Average 2015/20	**$5,200**	**$2,000**
Average 1995/00	**$700**	**$550**

C107 – Centenary of First International
Date of issue: 28 Sep, 1964

	Mint	**Used**
Europe	€75	€30
North America	$120	$25
East Asia	¥900	¥200
Southeast Asia	$130	$18
Average 2015/20	**$120**	**$30**
Average 1995/00	**$40**	**$10**

If you are going to buy this stamp from somewhere, investigate carefully and make sure the golden ink is not tarnished. Otherwise, the value would be no more than half of the price mentioned above.

Facts & Figures: First International

The First International (Official: International Workingmen's Association - IWA, 1864–1876) was founded in 1864 in Saint Martin's Hall, London. It is an international organization which aimed at uniting different socialist political groups and trade unions based on the working class and class struggle. George Odger, Henri Tolain and Edward Spencer Beesly are the key founders of the organization while Karl Marx is one of its key members. Its membership size is about 7-8 million.

C108 – 20th Anniversary of Albanian Liberation
Date of issue: 29 Nov, 1964

	Mint	Used
Europe	€100	€25
North America	$90	$30
East Asia	¥600	¥180
Southeast Asia	$85	$30
Average 2015/20	**$110**	**$30**
Average 1995/00	**$20**	**$10**

C109 – 30th Anniversary of the Zunyi Conference
Date of issue: 31 Jan, 1965

	Mint	Used
Europe	€200	€35
North America	$350	$100
East Asia	¥3,200	¥450
Southeast Asia	$420	$75
Average 2015/20	**$400**	**$75**
Average 1995/00	**$50**	**$30**

C113 – Socialist Countries' Postal Administrations Conference
Date of issue: 21 Jun, 1965

	Mint	Used
Europe	€30	€10
North America	$25	$7
East Asia	¥150	¥40
Southeast Asia	$24	$4
Average 2015/20	**$30**	**$9**
Average 1995/00	**$10**	**$2**

Insights: Related Issues

C113 of China is part of an omnibus issue, commemorating the Organization of Socialist Countries' Postal Administration Conference. Many of the countries share the uniform design, except for Czechoslovakia and Poland. Most countries issued a single-stamp set, except for Albania, with 2 denominations.

Collectors might be interested in this omnibus issue to accompany C113 in their collection. Currently, most of the stamps in this omnibus series are comparatively affordable. Most are sold in the market for a few cents to a few dollars (even in mint condition). Among all, the North Korean and Albanian issues would take a little bit extra effort to source.

Below are examples of other stamps in this omnibus issue:

Albania

Bulgaria

Czechoslovakia

DDR

Hungary

Mongolia

North Korea

North Vietnam

Poland

Romania

USSR

C116 – Second National Games
Date of issue: 28 Sep, 1965

	Mint	Used
Europe	€550	€25
North America	$500	$60
East Asia	¥3,500	¥400
Southeast Asia	$480	$78
Average 2015/20	**$600**	**$60**
Average 1995/00	**$200**	**$30**

C118 – Third Five-Year Plan
Date of issue: 15 Apr, 1967

	Mint	Used
Europe	€170	€45
North America	$180	$40
East Asia	¥1,000	¥300
Southeast Asia	$150	$32
Average 2015/20	**$190**	**$48**
Average 1995/00	**$70**	**$20**

C120 – Birth Centenary of Sun Yat-sen
Date of issue: 12 Nov, 1966

	Mint	Used
Europe	€100	€30
North America	$120	$30
East Asia	¥750	¥250
Southeast Asia	$90	$28
Average 2015/20	**$120**	**$36**
Average 1995/00	**$25**	**$5**

Insights: Thematic Collection

Dr. Sun Yat-sen is a wide theme to collect. 14 definitives issues of the Chinese Republic stamps already requires a lot of effort to collect, not to mention the surcharge issues (if you really want to venture into it). He is also featured in various stamps of Mainland China, Taiwan, Hong Kong and Macau after 1949. If you are into this theme, great! And all the best!

C121 – Cultural Revolution Games
Date of issue: 31 Dec, 1966

	Mint	Used
Europe	€300	€50
North America	$350	$80
East Asia	¥2,000	¥450
Southeast Asia	$300	$62
Average 2015/20	**$360**	**$75**
Average 1995/00	**$60**	**$20**

C122 – 30th Death Anniversary of Lu Xun
Date of issue: 31 Dec, 1966

	Mint	Used
Europe	€300	€90
North America	$350	$70
East Asia	¥2,000	¥500
Southeast Asia	$280	$62
Average 2015/20	**$350**	**$90**
Average 1995/00	**$100**	**$40**

Insights: Related Issues

If you collect this issue, you should look for other sets about Lu Xun as well: C11 (1951), C91 (1962), J11 (1976) & J67 (1981)... And don't forget to watch out for any new upcoming issues featuring this great writer!

C123 – Comrade Liu Yingjun
Date of issue: 25 Mar, 1967

	Mint	Used
Europe	€400	€100
North America	$350	$100
East Asia	¥2,200	¥750
Southeast Asia	$360	$95
Average 2015/20	**$420**	**$120**
Average 1995/00	**$120**	**$40**

Facts & Figures: Liu Yingjun

Liu Yingjun (Liu Ying Chun – 刘英俊, 1945 – 1966), was born in Jilin Province, from a poor peasant family. He joined the People's Liberation Army in 1962. In March 1966, he was riding the lead horse pulling a cannon. Frightened by the horn of a passing bus nearby, the horse was on the verge of running over the children on the roadside. Liu Yingjun managed to control the horse and save the children, but sacrificed his life due to the mortal injuries.

C124 – Heroic Oilwell Firefighters
Date of issue: 10 Mar, 1967

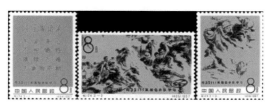

	Mint	Used
Europe	€180	€70
North America	$150	$75
East Asia	¥1,000	¥500
Southeast Asia	$180	$48
Average 2015/20	**$200**	**$78**
Average 1995/00	**$60**	**$20**

::: PRC S-Headed Issues :::

S1 – Chinese National Emblem
Date of issue: 1 Oct, 1951 | Date of reprint: 10 Jan, 1955

	Mint		Used	
	Original	Reprint	Original	Reprint
Europe	€60	€13	€25	€3
North America	$70	$20	$30	$12
East Asia	¥600	¥150	¥180	¥40
Southeast Asia	$80	$18	$16	$3
Average 2015/20	**$85**	**$20**	**$28**	**$7**
Average 1995/00	**$25**	**$3**	**$15**	**$2**

Insights: Differentiation between Original & Reprint

	Original	**Reprint**
1	Thicker paper	Whiter and thinner paper
2	The back of the stamps is flat	Embossed inscription can be observed at the back of the stamps

---

S2 – Agrarian Reform
Date of issue: 1 Jan, 1952; Date of reprint: 10 Jan, 1955

	Mint		**Used**	
	Original	**Reprint**	**Original**	**Reprint**
Europe	€30	€4	€12	€2
North America	$40	$8	$25	$4
East Asia	¥500	¥70	¥150	¥15
Southeast Asia	$42	$8	$30	$3
Average 2015/20	**$50**	**$8**	**$25**	**$3**
Average 1995/00	**$12**	**$2**	**$8**	**$1**

Insights: Differentiation between Original & Reprint

Original	**Reprint**
One line between the legs of the ploughman	Two lines between the legs of the ploughman

---

S4 – Gymnastics by Radio
Date of issue: 20 Jun, 1952 | Date of reprint: 10 Jan, 1955

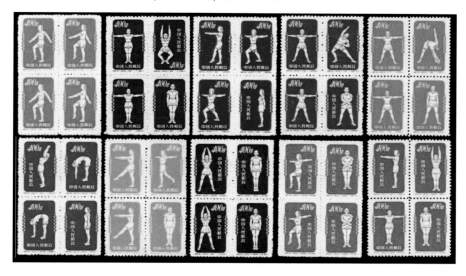

	Mint		Used	
	Original	**Reprint**	**Original**	**Reprint**
Europe	€1,200	€30	€1,200	€12
North America	$1,800	$50	$500	$45
East Asia	¥12,000	¥250	¥8,000	¥150
Southeast Asia	$1,600	$40	$1,600	$25
Average 2015/20	**$1,800**	**$45**	**$1,300**	**$28**
Average 1995/00	**$350**	**$20**	**$300**	**$10**

Insights: Differentiation between Original & Reprint

Original	**Reprint**
Thinner paper	Whiter and thicker paper, with fresher color

S15 – Views of Imperial Beijing
Date of issue: 1956-1957

	Mint	Used
Europe	€25	€2
North America	$40	$6
East Asia	¥200	¥40
Southeast Asia	$35	$4
Average 2015/20	**$36**	**$5**
Average 1995/00	**$12**	**$2**

Insights: Rarities

An unissued version exists for the (5-3) stamp, which shows beams of sunlight above Tiananmen Square. It was eventually redesigned to get rid of the so-called "nuclear glare". Nowadays, such a "nuclear glare" stamp will cost at least $145,000 (mint) or $70,000 (used), if ever come across.

Insights: Thematic

There are quite a lot of issues that you can collect under the buildings and monuments theme, not only PRC, but also Hong Kong, Macau and Taiwan. This issue is one of those. So far, there is not any issue that is too expensive to collect under this theme. But who knows what is going to happen in the future right?

S38 – Chinese Goldfish
Date of issue: 1 Jun, 1960

	Mint	Used
Europe	€500	€60
North America	$800	$100
East Asia	¥8,000	¥700
Southeast Asia	$800	$80
Average 2015/20	**$920**	**$100**
Average 1995/00	**$200**	**$60**

S40 – Pig Breeding
Date of issue: 15 Jun, 1960

	Mint	Used
Europe	€180	€10
North America	$300	$40
East Asia	¥1,800	¥250
Southeast Asia	$320	$45
Average 2015/20	**$300**	**$35**
Average 1995/00	**$70**	**$10**

S41 – Great Hall of the People
Date of issue: 1 Oct, 1960

	Mint	Used
Europe	€60	€12
North America	$100	$20
East Asia	¥750	¥200
Southeast Asia	$110	$40
Average 2015/20	**$100**	**$28**
Average 1995/00	**$25**	**$10**

S42 – New Railway Station of Beijing
Date of issue: 30 Aug, 1960

	Mint	Used
Europe	€70	€7
North America	$120	$20
East Asia	¥750	¥200
Southeast Asia	$110	$40
Average 2015/20	**$115**	**$26**
Average 1995/00	**$25**	**$10**

S44 – Chinese Chrysanthemums
Date of issue: 10 Dec, 1960

	Mint	Used
Europe	€500	€60
North America	$1,200	$120
East Asia	¥13,000	¥800
Southeast Asia	$1,800	$120
Average 2015/20	**$1,500**	**$120**
Average 1995/00	**$250**	**$70**

Insights: Thematic

There are quite a lot of issues that you can collect under the flowers theme. For PRC, these are some of the issues that you can take a look: Chrysanthemums (S44 – 1960), Peonies (S61 – 1964), Herbal flowers (T30 – 1978; T72 & T72M – 1982), Camellias (T37 – 1979), Lotus (T54 & T54M – 1980), Roses (T93 – 1984), Apricot Blossoms (T103 & T103M – 1985), Magnolias (T111 &T111M – 1986; 2005-5), Orchids (T129 & T129M – 1988), Narcissus (T147 – 1990), Rhododendron (T162 & T162M – 1991), Sweet Osmanthus (1995-6), Clivia (2000-14), Desert flowers (2002-14), Lily (2003-4 & 2003-4M), Peach Blossoms (2013-6), and many more that would be coming out in the future.

S46 – Tang Dynasty Pottery
Date of issue: 10 Nov, 1961

	Mint	Used
Europe	€200	€25
North America	$280	$40
East Asia	¥2,000	¥300
Southeast Asia	$300	$32
Average 2015/20	**$300**	**$40**
Average 1995/00	**$80**	**$40**

S47 – New Birth of Tibetan People
Date of issue: 20 Nov, 1961

	Mint	Used
Europe	€180	€15
North America	$350	$20
East Asia	¥2,500	¥200
Southeast Asia	$300	$30
Average 2015/20	**$330**	**$26**
Average 1995/00	**$70**	**$10**

S51 – Support for Cuba
Date of issue: 10 Jul, 1962

	Mint	Used
Europe	€200	€35
North America	$280	$65
East Asia	¥2,500	¥400
Southeast Asia	$300	$60
Average 2015/20	**$320**	**$60**
Average 1995/00	**$100**	**$30**

S56 - Butterflies
Date of issue: 5 Apr, 1963

	Mint	Used
Europe	€400	€35
North America	$450	$100
East Asia	¥3,500	¥500
Southeast Asia	$400	$70
Average 2015/20	**$500**	**$75**
Average 1995/00	**$200**	**$50**

S57 – Yellow Mountain (Huangshan)
Date of issue: 15 Oct, 1963

	Mint	Used
Europe	€800	€150
North America	$1,200	$200
East Asia	¥8,000	¥1,500
Southeast Asia	$1,300	$200
Average 2015/20	**$1,250**	**$220**
Average 1995/00	**$500**	**$120**

Facts & Figures: Huangshan

Located in southern Anhui, Huangshan is a famous mountain range that was recognized as a UNESCO World Heritage Site. It is one of China's major tourist destinations. The Huangshan mountain range has many peaks, some of which are more than 1,000 meters height. The site covers a core area of 154 square kilometers.

It is a frequent subject of poetry, paintings and photography, and of course, philately!!!

It is well-known for its sunrise, hot spring, "Buddha's light", pine trees and views of clouds from above. The site hosts millions of visitors from all over the world every year.

Insights: Thematic

Huangshan is the very first PRC issue that features the mountain scenery. That could be the reason why its value has appreciated so much. If you are collecting this theme, these following issues should also be included in the list: Mount Jingang (S73 – 1965), Guilin Landscapes (T53 – 1980), Stone Forrest (T64 – 1981), Mount Lu (T67 – 1981), Mount Emei (T100 – 1984), Mount Tai (T130 – 1988), Mount Hua (T140 – 1989), Mount Heng of Hunan (T155 – 1990), Mount Heng of Shanxi (T163 – 1991), Mount Changbai (1993-9), Mount Wuyi (1994-13), Mount Lu & Kumgang (1994-14), Three gorges of Yangtze river (1994-18), Mount Dinghu (1995-3), Mount Jiuhua (1995-20), Mount Song (1995-23), Mount Qingshan (1995-24), Heaven Mountain & Lake (1996-19), Mount Putuo (1996-6), Mount Huang (1997-16), Mount Lao (2000-14), Mount Wudang (2001-8), Mount Liupan (2001-25), Mount Qian (2002-8), Mount Yandang (2002-19), Mount Danxia (2004-8), Mount Jigong (2005-7), Mount Fanjing (2005-19), Mount Qingcheng (2006-7), Mount Tianzhu (2006-9), Tengchong Volcanoes (2007-23), Mount Fuchun paintings (2010-7), Mount Qingyuan (2015-14), and many more that will be issued in the future.

S59 – Giant Panda
Date of issue: 5 Aug, 1963

	Perforated		Imperforated	
	Mint	**Used**	**Mint**	**Used**
Europe	€120	€12	€350	€300
North America	$120	$10	$300	$130
East Asia	¥1,000	¥40	¥3,000	¥1,200
Southeast Asia	$140	$12	$400	$200
Average 2015/20	**$150**	**$12**	**$430**	**$250**
Average 1995/00	**$75**	**$10**	**$250**	**$120**

S60 – Golden-Haired Monkey
Date of issue: 25 Sep, 1963

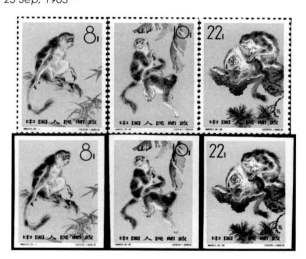

	Perforated		Imperforated	
	Mint	**Used**	**Mint**	**Used**
Europe	€45	€8	€200	€120
North America	$60	$10	$250	$100
East Asia	¥500	¥70	¥1,600	¥900
Southeast Asia	$70	$10	$280	$160
Average 2015/20	**$70**	**$10**	**$275**	**$150**
Average 1995/00	**$40**	**$10**	**$150**	**$60**

S61 & S61M – Chinese Peonies
Date of issue: Aug, 1964

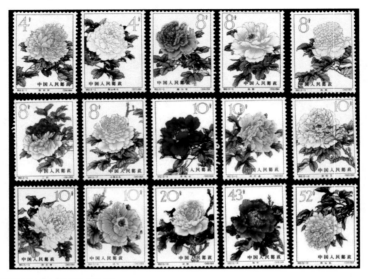

Stamps	Mint	Used
Europe	€450	€60
North America	$500	$100
East Asia	¥3,000	¥800
Southeast Asia	$550	$90
Average 2015/20	**$550**	**$100**
Average 1995/00	**$250**	**$80**

M/S	Mint	Used
Europe	€3,000	€1,200
North America	$2,800	$1,000
East Asia	¥17,000	¥8,000
Southeast Asia	$2,800	$1,300
Average 2015/20	**$3,200**	**$1,400**
Average 1995/00	**$1,000**	**$500**

S62 – New Industrial Machines
Date of issue: 30 Mar, 1966

	Mint	Used
Europe	€300	€25
North America	$320	$35
East Asia	¥1,800	¥300
Southeast Asia	$550	$90
Average 2015/20	**$400**	**$50**
Average 1995/00	**$100**	**$10**

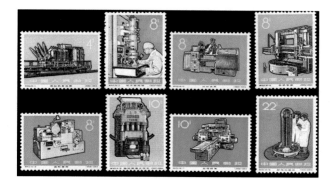

S63 – Bronze Vessels of the Yin Dynasty
Date of issue: 25 Aug, 1964

	Mint	Used
Europe	€120	€20
North America	$150	$30
East Asia	¥1,000	¥180
Southeast Asia	$190	$20
Average 2015/20	**$170**	**$28**
Average 1995/00	**$60**	**$10**

S65 – Shrine of the Chinese Revolution: Yan'an
Date of issue: 1 Jul, 1964

	Mint	Used
Europe	€120	€8
North America	$150	$25
East Asia	¥1,000	¥150
Southeast Asia	$150	$32
Average 2015/20	**$160**	**$25**
Average 1995/00	**$50**	**$10**

S67 – Petroleum Industry
Date of issue: 1 Oct, 1964

	Mint	Used
Europe	€400	€30
North America	$450	$60
East Asia	¥3,800	¥400
Southeast Asia	$580	$70
Average 2015/20	**$550**	**$60**
Average 1995/00	**$200**	**$20**

S68 – Hydro-Electric Power Station
Date of issue: 15 Dec, 1964

	Mint	Used
Europe	€350	€25
North America	$400	$45
East Asia	¥3,200	¥300
Southeast Asia	$480	$60
Average 2015/20	**$480**	**$50**
Average 1995/00	**$150**	**$15**

S70 – Chinese Mountaineering Achievements
Date of issue: 25 May, 1965

	Mint	Used
Europe	€60	€45
North America	$70	$25
East Asia	¥480	¥180
Southeast Asia	$85.00	$12.00
Average 2015/20	**$80**	**$30**
Average 1995/00	**$25**	**$6**

S73 – Cradle of the Chinese Revolution: Jingang Mountains
Date of issue: 1 Jul, 1965

	Mint	Used
Europe	€250	€25
North America	$250	$50
East Asia	¥2,300	¥300
Southeast Asia	$320	$50
Average 2015/20	**$330**	**$48**
Average 1995/00	**$100**	**$10**

S74 – People's Liberation Army
Date of issue: 1 Aug, 1965

	Mint	Used
Europe	€350	€55
North America	$380	$80
East Asia	¥2,500	¥500
Southeast Asia	$350	$70
Average 2015/20	**$420**	**$78**
Average 1995/00	**$100**	**$20**

::: PRC W-Headed Issues :::

Between 1966 and 1976, there was a social-political movement in China known as the Cultural Revolution, initiated by Mao Zedong. Its objective was to preserve true Communist ideology and to re-impose the dominant role of Maoism in the Party.

As part of the movement, stamp collecting was banned in China since it was considered as a bourgeois pursuit. Recently, there has been increasing interest in stamps of the Cultural Revolution era, driving its price to the new record globally. All high value issues will be introduced in this part.

W1 – Thoughts of Chairman Mao (1st Issue)
Date of issue: 20 Apr, 1967

	Se-tenant Strips		Separate Stamps	
	Mint	**Used**	**Mint**	**Used**
Europe	€5,000	€1,200	€2,000	€750
North America	$6,000	$1,600	$1,200	$900
East Asia	¥30,000	¥9,000	¥10,000	¥5,000
Southeast Asia	$7,500	$1,500	$2,950	$430
Average 2015/20	**$6,500**	**$1,600**	**$2,200**	**$830**
Average 1995/00	**$700**	**$200**	**$300**	**$120**

Again, do make sure the golden ink is not tarnished if you intend to add this set to your collection. Otherwise, the value would differ significantly.

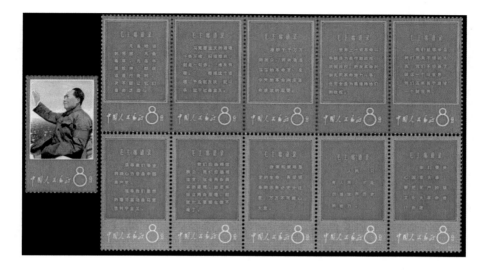

W2 – Long Live Chairman Mao
Date of issue: 1 May, 1967

	Mint	Used
Europe	€2,500	€350
North America	$1,700	$650
East Asia	¥15,000	¥4,000
Southeast Asia	$2,000	$600
Average 2015/20	**$2,500**	**$600**
Average 1995/00	**$400**	**$120**

W3 – "Talks at the Yan'an Forum on Literature and Art" 25th Anniversary
Date of issue: 23 May, 1967

	Mint	Used
Europe	£1,500	£400
North America	$1,200	$500
East Asia	¥8,000	¥3,000
Southeast Asia	$1,200	$450
Average 2015/20	**$1,400**	**$500**
Average 1995/00	**$450**	**$50**

W4 – 46th Anniversary of Chinese Communist Party
Date of issue: 1 Jul, 1967

	Mint	Used
Europe	€450	€100
North America	$450	$120
East Asia	¥4,000	¥800
Southeast Asia	$500	$160
Average 2015/20	**$570**	**$140**
Average 1995/00	**$200**	**$80**

W5 – Revolutionary Literature & Art
Date of issue: 1968-1969

	Mint	Used
Europe	€2,000	€250
North America	$1,500	$450
East Asia	¥15,000	¥3,000
Southeast Asia	$1,500	$540
Average 2015/20	**$2,100**	**$460**
Average 1995/00	**$300**	**$60**

W6 – 18th Anniversary of the People's Republic
Date of issue: 1 Oct, 1967

	Mint	Used
Europe	€300	€80
North America	$280	$120
East Asia	¥2,000	¥700
Southeast Asia	$230	$100
Average 2015/20	**$320**	**$115**
Average 1995/00	**$50**	**$10**

W7 – Poems of Chairman Mao
Date of issue: 1967-1968

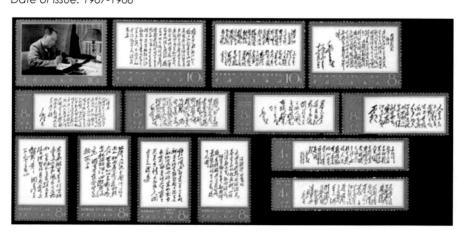

	Mint	Used
Europe	€4,000	€1,200
North America	$4,200	$1,400
East Asia	¥30,000	¥10,000
Southeast Asia	$4,500	$1,500
Average 2015/20	**$5,000**	**$1,600**
Average 1995/00	**$700**	**$150**

Insights: Related Issues

A North Korean issue featuring Mao Zedong's poems (2013)

A Mali issue featuring Mao Zedong's poems (2013)

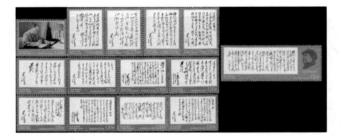

A Guinea-Bissau issue featuring Mao Zedong's poems (2013)

A Liberia issue featuring Mao Zedong's poems (2013)

A Sierra Leone issue featuring Mao Zedong's poems (2013)

W9 – Chairman Mao's Anti-American Declaration
Date of issue: 13 May, 1968

	Mint	Used
Europe	€350	€80
North America	$300	$120
East Asia	¥3,200	¥750
Southeast Asia	$400	$120
Average 2015/20	**$440**	**$120**
Average 1995/00	**$50**	**$10**

W10 – Directives of Chairman Mao
Date of issue: 20 Jul, 1968

	Se-tenant Strips		Separate Stamps	
	Mint	Used	Mint	Used
Europe	€6,000	€2,000	€1,800	€800
North America	$7,500	$3,000	$2,800	$1,200
East Asia	¥55,000	¥20,000	$18,000	¥7,000
Southeast Asia	$7,600	$2,800	$1,000	$500
Average 2015/20	**$8,300**	**$3,000**	**$2,400**	**$1,000**
Average 1995/00	**$1,200**	**$300**	**$400**	**$80**

W12 – Chairman Mao en route to Anyuan
Date of issue: 1 Aug, 1968

	Mint	Used
Europe	€180	€40
North America	$200	$50
East Asia	¥1,500	¥400
Southeast Asia	$250	$40
Average 2015/20	**$240**	**$50**
Average 1995/00	**$20**	**$8**

Facts & Figures: Chairman Mao en route to Anyuan

Chairman Mao en route to Anyuan is an oil painting by Liu Chunhua in the 1950s. It pictures a young Mao Zedong as one of the common people, ready to take on any obstacle that comes forth. This artwork is a strong example of Chinese communist propaganda and shows the devotion which their culture had to Chairman Mao.

The painting has been reproduced over nine hundred million times, and distributed widely in print, sculpture, and other media.

Anyuan is a district in the south of Jiangxi province, in which the Anyuan Miners' Strike took place in 1922. This is considered an important event to the Chinese Communist Party during its first days.

Insights: Related Issues

North Korea, Liberia and Ivory Coast issues using the same materials as W12.

There are 2 North Korea issues using this design: 2011 and 2013. The 2011 issue is a single-stamp issue, while the 2013 stamp belongs to a set with 16 values that we are going to look at later.

The Ivory Coast set has 10 values.

The Liberia stamp is part of a miniature sheet with 4 stamps on it,

W13 – Thoughts of Chairman Mao (2nd Issue)
Date of issue: 15 Aug, 1968

	Mint	Used
Europe	€200	€60
North America	$250	$60
East Asia	¥1,500	¥400
Southeast Asia	$250	$50
Average 2015/20	**$260**	**$70**
Average 1995/00	**$25**	**$5**

Insights: Related Issues

There's also a North Korean issue in 2013, adopting the Chinese W series designs. This is to commemorate 120th anniversary of Mao Zedong's birthday. You can consider collecting these stamps to accompany your W series collection. The set has 16 values, and the size of the stamps is smaller than their original counterparts.

W15 – The Words of Chairman Mao
Date of issue: 26 Dec, 1968

	Mint	Used
Europe	€80	€30
North America	$70	$20
East Asia	¥600	¥200
Southeast Asia	$85	$15.00
Average 2015/20	**$95**	**$28**
Average 1995/00	**$10**	**$3**

W16 – Piano Music from "The Red Lantern"
Date of issue: 1 Aug, 1969

	Mint	Used
Europe	€150	€30
North America	$140	$35
East Asia	¥1,000	¥280
Southeast Asia	$140	$25
Average 2015/20	**$170**	**$38**
Average 1995/00	**$40**	**$15**

Facts & Figures: The Legend of the Red Lantern

The Legend of the Red Lantern (红灯记) is one of the revolutionary operas (or model operas) during the Chinese Cultural Revolution. These are only operas and ballets permitted during this period of time.

The play focuses on the communist underground activities during the Japanese occupation in 1939, involving three young women who are determined to join the revolutionary force and carry the revolution to the end. They exhibited the extreme anger and hatred towards their enemies.

W18 – Defense of Zhenbao Island (Damansky Island)
Date of issue: 1 Oct, 1969

	Mint	Used
Europe	€150	€50
North America	$130	$45
East Asia	¥900	¥300
Southeast Asia	$120	$30
Average 2015/20	**$160**	**$50**
Average 1995/00	**$30**	**$20**

Facts & Figures: The Sino-Soviet Border Conflict in 1969

The Sino-Soviet border conflict was a seven-month undeclared military conflict between the Soviet Union and China in 1969. The border issues were not resolved until the 1991 Sino-Soviet Border Agreement, although military conflict has ceased that year. The most serious of these border clashes happened in March 1969 in the vicinity of Zhenbao Island on the Ussuri River.

About 150 casualties were reported from the Soviet side, while there's no alignment in the number of Chinese casualties. China claimed that 71 were killed and 68 wounded on their side, while Soviet reported 800 deaths from their rivals.

W19 – Heroic Death of Jin Xunhua in Jilin Border Flood
Date of issue: 21 Jan, 1970

	Mint	Used
Europe	€50	€25
North America	$35	$18
East Asia	¥280	¥120
Southeast Asia	$40	$10
Average 2015/20	**$50**	**$20**
Average 1995/00	**$15**	**$5**

Insights: Variations

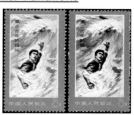

Two different versions exist for this issue, one known as "black water" and the other, "white water". The value computed above is meant for the "white water" version. There's a slight price difference between these two versions – a discrepancy of under $10.

Withdrawn Issue – The Whole Country is Red
Date of issue: 25 Nov, 1968

The stamp features a red map of China and a worker, a farmer and a soldier holding the red book. The Chinese words on the map read "The Whole Country is Red". However, Taiwan was not shaded with red in the stamp. The stamps were withdrawn within half a day and most of them were destroyed. Only a small quantity of the stamp went to private collections. The stamp has been sold in various auctions and realized at high price, for example, $480,000 in 2009 in Hong Kong; $45,000 in 2010 in UK; $96,000 in 2011 in Hong Kong; $57,000 in 2014 in Germany, $445,000 in 2014 in Hong Kong. The catalogue value of the stamps is in the range of $200,000 (mint) and $100,000 (used).

Unissued Stamps – Great Victory of Cultural Revolution

The two values below was prepared to commemorate the victory of the Cultural Revolution, but not issued. A few examples managed to enter the marketplace.

The first stamp featuring Mao Zedong and Marshall Lin Biao. Its catalogue value is in the range of $300,000. The stamp was sold at $324,000 in an auction in 2011.

The second stamp is the larger version of "The Whole Country is Red". It was sold in an auction at $1.15 million in 2014. The catalogue value of the stamps is in the range of $1,000,000.

Insights: Related Issues

It is interesting to see other countries adopting the designs of rare China stamps for their official issues. Below is another issue by Guinea-Bissau.

The stamp was issued in 2013, as part of the commemorative series for Mao Zedong's 120th birthday.

Unissued Stamps – The Great Blue Sky

The catalogue value of the stamps is in the range of $400,000.

Unissued Stamp – Mao Zedong's Inscription for the Japanese Workforce

The catalogue value of the stamp is in the range of $150,000. A block of 4 was sold for $1.15 million in 2011, setting the world record price for red China stamps.

::: PRC Numbered Issues :::

#1-6 – Revolutionary Opera "Taking Tiger Mountain"
Date of issue: 1 Aug, 1970

	Mint	Used
Europe	€200	€50
North America	$250	$60
East Asia	¥1,600	¥300
Southeast Asia	$50	$10
Average 2015/20	**$220**	**$48**
Average 1995/00	**$50**	**$15**

Facts & Figures: Taking Tiger Mountain by Strategy

Taking Tiger Mountain by Strategy (智取威虎山) is another model plays during the Chinese Cultural Revolution. The story is based on a real-life incident in 1946 during the Chinese Civil War, involving a communist reconnaissance team soldier Yang Zirong who disguised himself as a bandit to infiltrate a local gang of bandits, eventually helping the Communist force to destroy the bandits.

#8-11 – Centenary of Paris Commune
Date of issue: 18 Mar, 1971

	Mint	Used
Europe	€380	€100
North America	$400	$120
East Asia	¥3,200	¥700
Southeast Asia	$530	$100
Average 2015/20	**$500**	**$120**
Average 1995/00	**$120**	**$50**

#12-20 – 50th Anniversary of Communist Party of China
Date of issue: 1 Jul, 1971

	Mint	Used
Europe	€280	€60
North America	$400	$60
East Asia	¥3,500	¥400
Southeast Asia	$680	$80
Average 2015/20	**$520**	**$75**
Average 1995/00	**$60**	**$20**

#33-38 – 30th Anniversary of the Publication of the Discussions on Literature and Art at the Yan'an Forum
Date of issue: 23 May, 1972

	Mint	Used
Europe	€120	€40
North America	$150	$45
East Asia	¥1,000	¥250
Southeast Asia	$150	$40
Average 2015/20	**$160**	**$45**
Average 1995/00	**$40**	**$10**

#53-56 – Revolutionary Ballet "White-Haired Girl"
Date of issue: 25 Sep, 1973

	Mint	Used
UK	€120	€35
US	$200	$50
China	¥1,200	¥300
Singapore	$150	$30
Average 2015/16	**$180**	**$45**
Average 1995/96	**$20**	**$5**

Facts & Figures: The White-Haired Girl

The White-Haired Girl (白毛女) is another model play allowed during the Chinese Cultural Revolution period. The story depicts the misery suffered by local peasantry of the Shanxi, Chahar and Hebei during the late Qing dynasty to 1930s, when the Japanese troops invaded China. The main character is Xi'er, a peasant girl who ran away from the landlord and lived in the cave to escape from being his concubine. Her hair turned white due to the hardship. In the end, Xi'er's fiancé joined the Eighth Route Army and fought the Japanese invaders. He returned to the village to overthrow the rule of the landlord. They distribute the farmland to the peasants. He went and looked for Xi'er in the mountains and they finally reunited.

#57-62 – Giant Panda
Date of issue: 15 Jan, 1973

	Mint	Used
Europe	€200	€65
North America	$180	$60
East Asia	¥1,000	¥400
Southeast Asia	$280	$70
Average 2015/20	**$230**	**$75**
Average 1995/00	**$100**	**$50**

#78-81 – Industrial Productions
Date of issue: 23 Dec, 1974

	Mint	Used
Europe	€400	€150
North America	$600	$100
East Asia	¥3,800	¥750
Southeast Asia	$420	$100
Average 2015/20	**$560**	**$140**
Average 1995/00	**$60**	**$25**

::: PRC J-Headed Issues :::

J8 – Fulfillment of 4th Five-Year Plan
Date of issue: 9 Apr, 1976

	Mint	Used
Europe	€180	€30
North America	$200	$45
East Asia	¥1,200	¥300
Southeast Asia	$200	$40
Average 2015/20	**$220**	**$45**
Average 1995/00	**$60**	**$25**

J41 – 31st International Stamp Exhibition in Italy
Date of issue: 25 Aug, 1979

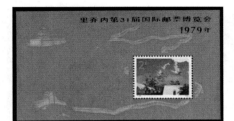

	Mint	Used
Europe	€800	€300
North America	$750	$280
East Asia	¥4,500	¥1,800
Southeast Asia	$680	$250
Average 2015/20	**$850**	**$320**
Average 1995/00	**$400**	**$200**

J42 – People's Republic of China Philatelic Exhibition
Date of issue: 10 Nov, 1979

	Mint	Used
Europe	€550	€200
North America	$450	$150
East Asia	¥2,600	¥1,500
Southeast Asia	$380	$100
Average 2015/20	**$520**	**$200**
Average 1995/00	**$200**	**$80**

The value indicated above is for MS with numbers and overprints in gold. Normal print (for mint MS) will be about half of the value.

J58 – Ancient Chinese Scientists (3rd Issue)
Date of issue: 20 Nov, 1980

	Mint	Used
Europe	€60	€12
North America	$70	$15
East Asia	¥500	¥100
Southeast Asia	$55	$15
Average 2015/20	**$75**	**$16**
Average 1995/00	**$13**	**$6**

Insights: Related Issues

Three different issues of the Ancient Chinese Scientists series have been introduced in this chapter. If you collect this series, don't forget to grasp the 4th issue (2002-18) that is still very affordable nowadays, and watch out for any 5th, 6th and etc. issues that might be coming out in the future.

There are also the Modern Chinese Scientists series that you can collect to accompany this series: J149 (1988), J173 (1990), 1992-19, 2006-11 (price is on the rise), 2011-14, 2014-25, 2016-11.

A few other issues relating to science and invention can also be considered to add into this topic: China S7 (1953), China Macau Great Inventions (2005), China Hong Kong Great Inventions (2005), China Hong Kong's Scientists Issue (2015).

::: PRC T-Headed Issues :::

T28 & T28M – Galloping Horses
Date of issue: 5 May, 1978

	Stamp Set		Miniature Sheet	
	Mint	**Used**	**Mint**	**Used**
Europe	€60	€15	€500	€180
North America	$90	$25	$600	$200
East Asia	¥500	¥150	¥4,500	¥1,200
Southeast Asia	$70	$10	$600	$80
Average 2015/20	**$80**	**$20**	**$680**	**$190**
Average 1995/00	**$15**	**$8**	**$150**	**$70**

T41M – Study Science from Childhood
Date of issue: 3 Oct, 1979

	Mint	Used
Europe	€2,000	€900
North America	$2,000	$1,200
East Asia	¥15,000	¥10,000
Southeast Asia	$1,800	$200
Average 2015/20	**$2,300**	**$1,100**
Average 1995/00	**$500**	**$200**

T43 – The Journey to the West
Date of issue: 1 Dec, 1979

	Mint	Used
Europe	€60	€15
North America	$90	$25
East Asia	¥600	¥150
Southeast Asia	$70	$20
Average 2015/20	**$90**	**$25**
Average 1995/00	**$25**	**$10**

We'll revisit this set in another section of this chapter on thematic collection.

T44 & T44M – Qi Baishi Paintings
Date of issue: 15 Jan, 1980

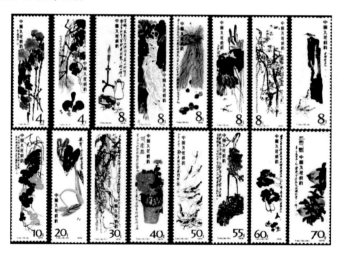

Stamps Set	Mint	Used
Europe	€120	€25
North America	$140	$35
East Asia	¥900	¥200
Southeast Asia	$140	$30
Average 2015/20	**$150**	**$35**
Average 1995/00	**$25**	**$10**

M/S	Mint	Used
Europe	€300	€120
North America	$350	$140
East Asia	¥2,000	¥900
Southeast Asia	$320	$150
Average 2015/20	**$360**	**$160**
Average 1995/00	**$70**	**$30**

Facts & Figures: Qi Baishi

Qi Baishi (齐白石, 1864 – 1957) is a renown Chinese painter. He has produced more than 10,000 distinct works throughout his life, 3,000 of which can be found in museums nowadays. Many of his works have also been auctioned, one of which realized at about $65 million and became the most expensive paintings ever being sold in auctions.

Insights: Thematic

Chinese painting theme is a very wide topic. It covers quite a number of issues ranging from Mainland China to Hong Kong, Macau and Taiwan. We'll talk about Chinese painting theme in the next few sections of this chapter. In the meantime, I just want to highlight that this theme takes a lot of time and effort if you want to venture into it. If you want to pursue this theme, set aside some significant budget too.

T45 – Chinese Opera Masks
Date of issue: 25 Jan, 1980

	Mint	Used
Europe	€50	€15
North America	$60	$20
East Asia	¥300	¥120
Southeast Asia	$50	$16
Average 2015/20	**$60**	**$20**
Average 1995/00	**$20**	**$10**

Insights: Rarities

A set of eight stamps similar to T45 was prepared but not issued in 1964, with the year "1964" being displayed instead of 1980, and it should have been indexed as S62 (特62) if it had been issued 16 years earlier. These are very rare and are currently selling at minimum $125,000 if to be come across.

We'll revisit this set in another section of this chapter when discussing about Chinese performing arts theme.

T46 – Year of the Monkey
Date of issue: 15 Feb, 1980

	Mint	Used
Europe	€1,600	€750
North America	$2,200	$650
East Asia	¥12,500	¥4,800
Southeast Asia	$1,900	$900
Average 2015/20	**$2,200**	**$870**
Average 1995/00	**$120**	**$50**

Insights: The Most Famous China Stamp

The Monkey stamp of 1980 is one of the most sought after modern Chinese stamp in the history. It is not rare, but millions of people are hunting for it, driving the market price of a fine copy to thousands of dollars. A full sheet of 80 of such stamp was sold at $180,000 during an auction in 2011.

We'll revisit this stamp in the upcoming section of the chapter on Zodiac stamp collection.

T69 & T69M – Twelve Beauties of the Dream of Red Mansions
Date of issue: 20 Nov, 1981

	Mint	Stamp Set Used	Mint	Miniature Sheet Used
Europe	€50	€15	€200	€90
North America	$65	$18	$250	$120
East Asia	¥450	¥120	¥1,500	¥700
Southeast Asia	$65	$20	$220	$100
Average 2015/20	**$70**	**$20**	**$255**	**$120**
Average 1995/00	**$15**	**$8**	**$30**	**$20**

Again, we'll revisit this set in the next section of this chapter discussing thematic collection.

::: PRC Year Issues :::

For the time being, issues from 1992 onwards haven't seen any unusual price increase yet. Most of the issues are quite affordable. I just want to highlight a few issues that have risen to a relatively high value compared to their issuing price, as a consequence of the recent mass disassembling of stamp sheets, and also speculation from Mainland China and Hong Kong.

Pay close attention to the following issues:

- 1997-10: Return of Hong Kong to China (especially the gold foiled MS)
- 1999-11: 50th Anniversary of the PRC (sheetlet of 56 stamps)
- 1999-18: Return of Macau to China (especially the gold foiled MS)
- 2002-5: "The Royal Carriage" Painting
- 2003-7: Leshan Giant Buddha
- 2003-25: 110th Birth Anniversary of Comrade Mao Zedong
- 2004-15: Eight Immortals Crossing the Sea
- 2005-25: River Luo Goddess Painting
- 2006-14: Early Leaders of the Chinese Communist Party (2nd issue)
- 2006-18: 140th Birth Anniversary of Dr. Sun Yat-sen
- 2006-30: Harmonious Railway Construction
- 2006-31: Birth Centenary Anniversary of Comrade Ulanhu
- 2013-8M: Beating White Silk Painting
- 2013-30: 120th Birth Anniversary of Comrade Mao Zedong
- 2014-4M: "Bathing Horses" Painting
- 2015-5M: "Court Ladies Wielding Fans" Painting

Speculators also like to keep sheetlets and whole panes of their favorite issues. Nowadays, China stamp sheets have become smaller, easier to maintain, cheaper to buy and can mark-up higher when resell. We usually call these "mini-panes".

For China stamps, each mini-pane carries only one value, while Macau will usually have the whole set on one single mini-pane.

::: PRC Military Stamps :::

There are only 2 military issues produced by the People's Republic of China. The first issue of 1953 is quite rare and valuable.

These stamps were designed and issued free-of-charge to the soldiers who were on active duty, so that they can use them to send letters.
Shortly after the stamps were issued, the Army realized that they might face a risk of confidential information being leaked out, especially from the letters using such stamps. As a consequence, all stamps were ordered to be returned and destroyed. A small number of them still survive until today.

The blue stamp is the rarest among those three. It yielded closed to $430,000 in an auction in 2011.

::: Republic of China (Taiwan) :::

Early issues of Taiwan after 1949 are quite valuable, especially those mint stamps and miniature sheets. This section will highlight some of these good sets.

Def.75 – Zheng Chenggong (Koxinga)
Date of issue: 26 Jun, 1950

Com.32 & Com.33 – Commemoration of Self-Governing Districts
Date of issue: 20 Mar, 1951

This issue comes with a perforated set, an imperforated and a miniature sheet. Price of the imperforated set and the miniature sheet are much higher.

Com.34 – Land Tax Reduction
Date of issue: 1 Jan, 1952

This set was also issued with perforated and imperforated versions. The price of the imperforated set is at least twice as much of the perforated.

Com.35 – 2nd Anniversary of Chiang Kai-shek's Re-election as President
Date of issue: 1 Mar, 1952

Com.36 – 3rd Anniversary of Chiang Kai-shek's Re-election as President
Date of issue: 1 Mar, 1953

Def.80 – President Chiang Kai-shek
Date of issue: 31 Oct, 1952

*
* *

The later issues are currently quite affordable and collectors should be able to get them at good price, since the demand for Taiwan stamps is yet to be as high as PRC, Qing dynasty and Hong Kong stamps. There are various miniature sheets issued during this period to collect; and they seem to catch up faster in value.

A number of Chinese painting stamps were issued after 1960, and they are catching up in demand. Below are a few examples:

Sp.27 – Ancient Chinese Emperors Paintings
Date of issue: 20 Sep, 1962

This is one of the most expensive contemporary Taiwan stamp sets. A mint set currently costs a few hundred dollars and the value is increasing.

This set features the founding Emperors of four great Chinese dynasties: Tang (唐), Song (宋), Yuan (元) and Ming (明).

Sp.80 – The Ten Prized Dogs Paintings
Date of issue: 16 Nov, 1971

Sp.97 & Sp.97a – The Eight Prized Horses Paintings
Date of issue: 21 Oct, 1973

The Eight Prized Horses set is much cheaper than the other two sets. But lately it is drawing so much attention of collectors worldwide. Bidding wars were happening quite aggressively on eBay. People visiting stamp shops were asking for it quite often. The issue also comes with a miniature sheet containing 4 stamps.

There are various themes in Taiwan stamps that collectors can choose to focus on: Chinese paintings, ancient arts treasures, famous people of the ancient and modern time, Chinese myths & folk tales, Chinese literature, birds, flowers, Chiang Kai-shek, Chinese Zodiac etc. In general, Taiwan philately is another interesting area that is worth exploring.

::: Hong Kong :::

When it comes to modern Hong Kong stamps, various QEII definitives issues are worth considering. If you are collecting these, try to get the mint stamps instead of used.

Collectors and speculators are also interested in some modern Hong Kong stamps, especially Zodiac issues. We'll talk about this in due time.

::: Macau :::

Modern Macau stamps started to become more and more popular in the market lately, especially after the major speculation activities from Mainland collectors in 2016. Zodiac and Chinese classical literature are the two themes that experienced significant rise in value. Most sets would be issued in mini-panes that consist of a few complete sets. So, each the complete set would be available in se-tenant blocks or strips.

Many collectors would prefer to keep mini-panes over one se-tenant blocks or strips of complete set. Most speculators will just keep mini-panes and miniature sheets.

D. Thematic Collection

::: Zodiac :::

Since the surge in price of the Monkey stamp (T46), Zodiac has become an evergreen topic and the apple of many collectors' eye.

Though Mainland China is not the very first to issue Zodiac stamps (it is indeed started in Japan, dated back to 1950), Zodiac stamps from China are among the most sought-after, followed by Hong Kong and Macau. More and more countries are issuing regular Zodiac stamps nowadays, with increasingly diverse design.

If you are into this theme, be ready to set aside significant budget. T46 alone will cost you almost 20 years of a single country's annual stamp collection.

However, this is a very exciting theme. Venturing into this area means every year you have something to look forward to. And remember to buy the stamps when they are newly released. You will never know how volatile they become after a while.

Now, let's take a closer look at all Zodiac stamps in the Chinese philately domain.

Mainland China

We looked into T46 before. Now let's look at the rest of the stamps in the first Zodiac cycle of PRC stamps. Besides the famous Monkey stamp that cost an arm and leg, the Rooster (1981) that cost about $40 and the Pig (1983) that cost about $15, the rest of the stamps in this cycle can be sourced at less than $10.

Besides collecting the individual stamps, a few collectors are collecting pairs, block of four, and many collectors are collecting full sheets of 80 stamps. (Of course not many of us can do that with T46)

| T46: 1980 Monkey | T58: 1981 Rooster | T70: 1982 Dog | T80: 1983 Pig |

| T90: 1984 Rat | T102: 1985 Ox | T107: 1986 Tiger | T112: 1987 Rabbit |

| T124: 1988 Dragon | T133: 1989 Snake | T146: 1990 Horse | T159: 1991 Sheep |

Each issue in the second cycle consists of 2 values. Most issues can be sourced at $5 or below, except for the Dragon issue (2000), which can cost over $20. These stamps are issued in full sheet of 40, or sheetlets of 6 stamps (for each value).

| 1992-1: Monkey | 1993-1: Rooster | 1994-1: Dog |

| 1995-1: Pig | 1996-1: Rat | 1997-1: Ox |

1998-1: Tiger   1999-1: Rabbit   2000-1: Dragon

2001-1: Snake   2002-1: Horse   2003-1: Sheep

The third cycle comprises 12 single-value issues. Stamps are issued in panes of 20 (or 24 stamps in the case of Monkey 2004 and Rooster 2005), sheetlets of 6, gift sheetlets of 4 (yellow color), or booklets of 10.

You can buy most of the stamps in this series at $5 or below. Be aware that stamps from booklet don't have the serial numbers when you view them under UV lights. Try to collect those with serial numbers because they worth much more.

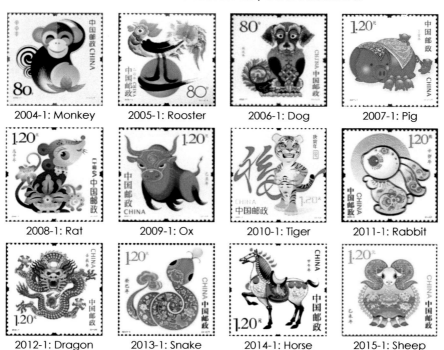

2004-1: Monkey   2005-1: Rooster   2006-1: Dog   2007-1: Pig

2008-1: Rat   2009-1: Ox   2010-1: Tiger   2011-1: Rabbit

2012-1: Dragon   2013-1: Snake   2014-1: Horse   2015-1: Sheep

Full pane

Sheetlet (White)

Gift Sheetlet (Yellow)

Booklet

Currently, PRC Zodiac stamps are running in the fourth cycle (2016 to 2027). Each issue has 2 values. Again, stamps are also available in full panes of 16, sheetlets of 6 (for each value), and booklets of 10 (5 stamps for each value), and gift sheetlets of 4 (2 stamps for each value).

Hong Kong

Hong Kong started issuing the first Zodiac issue in 1967. Each issue in this cycle consists of two values. Currently, the average market price of the full cycle is about $300 (mint)/ $150 (used).

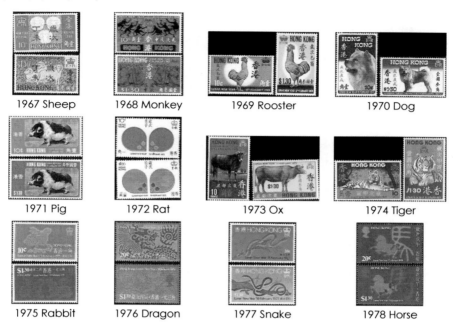

1967 Sheep	1968 Monkey	1969 Rooster	1970 Dog
1971 Pig	1972 Rat	1973 Ox	1974 Tiger
1975 Rabbit	1976 Dragon	1977 Snake	1978 Horse

Between 1979 and 1986, Hong Kong didn't issue New Year greeting stamps. The second cycle was resumed in 1987 after 8 years of interruption.

The second cycle consists of 12 four-value issues. Each issue also comes with a miniature sheet with the exact 4 stamps in the set.

| 1987 Rabbit | 1988 Dragon |

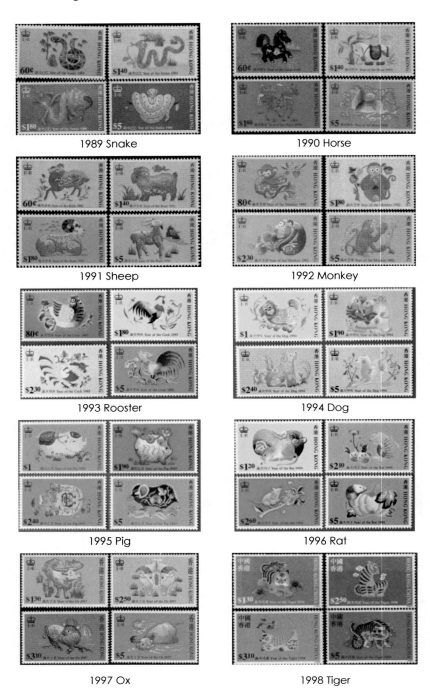

1989 Snake

1990 Horse

1991 Sheep

1992 Monkey

1993 Rooster

1994 Dog

1995 Pig

1996 Rat

1997 Ox

1998 Tiger

The official third cycle, made up of 12 four-value issues, somehow started in 2000, making 1999's Rabbit an odd issue. Each issue comes with a miniature sheet with the exact 4 stamps in the set, and an imperforated miniature sheet, denominated at HK$5. Besides, there's also a "Gold & Silver" miniature sheet denominated at HK$100.

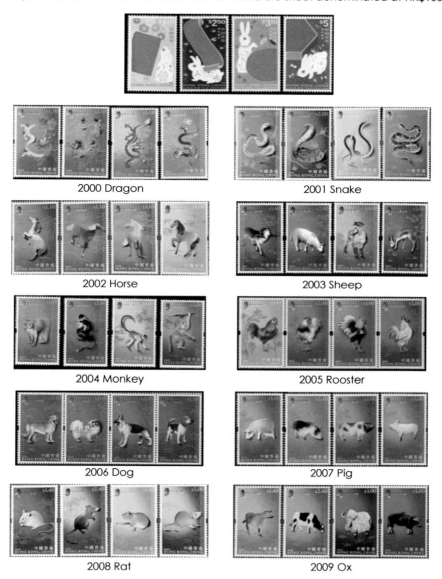

2000 Dragon   2001 Snake

2002 Horse   2003 Sheep

2004 Monkey   2005 Rooster

2006 Dog   2007 Pig

2008 Rat   2009 Ox

2010 Tiger   2011 Rabbit

The fourth cycle, again, consisting of four-value issues, started in 2012. Each comes with a miniature sheet with HK$10 face value and a silk miniature sheet nominated at HK$50. There is a Certificate of Authenticity issued with each silk miniature sheet.

Macau

Macau started the latest among the four. The first issue dated back in 1984. The first cycle ran from 1984 to 1995.

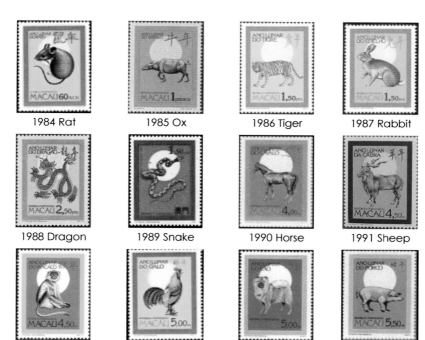

| 1984 Rat | 1985 Ox | 1986 Tiger | 1987 Rabbit |

| 1988 Dragon | 1989 Snake | 1990 Horse | 1991 Sheep |

| 1992 Monkey | 1993 Rooster | 1994 Dog | 1995 Pig |

... Followed by the second cycle, which comes with a 12 single-value issues at MOP$5.50 each, and also a miniature sheet at MOP$10 each.

| 1996 Rat | 1997 Ox | 1998 Tiger | 1999 Rabbit |

| S002: 2000 Dragon | S013: 2001 Snake | S026: 2002 Horse | S039: 2003 Sheep |

| S050: 2004 Monkey | S061: 2005 Rooster | S073: 2006 Dog | S084: 2007 Pig |

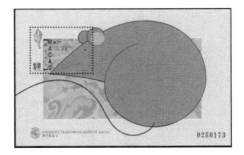

The third cycle is currently running and finishing. Each set comprises 5 values in se-tenant strips and a miniature sheet denominated MOP$10.

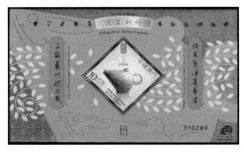

Taiwan

Among the four, Taiwan is currently leading in the amount of issues, mainly because it started quite early. Although Taiwan's inception is 2 years later than Hong Kong, there's been no interruption since 1969. Stamps are usually issued in December of the previous year, unlike other countries (January of the New Year itself). Currently, collectors don't really need to spend a lot of money in this area. The first cycle consists of 11 two-value sets and an eight-value set in two se-tenant blocks (for Rat year 1972). The most expensive issue in this cycle is Rooster 1969 (over $50), Rat 1972 (about $30). The rest generally cost somewhere between $2 and $10.

Sp.55: 1969 Rooster

Sp.62: 1970 Dog

Sp.74: 1971 Pig

Sp.81: 1972 Rat   Sp.89: 1973 Ox   Sp.98: 1974 Tiger

Sp.107: 1975 Rabbit   Sp.119: 1976 Dragon   Sp.126: 1977 Snake

Sp.138: 1978 Horse   Sp.147: 1979 Sheep   Sp.158: 1980 Monkey

There are 12 two-value issues in the second cycle, and 12 miniature sheets of 4 stamps (two similar sets from the main issue). All of the issues follow the same motif.

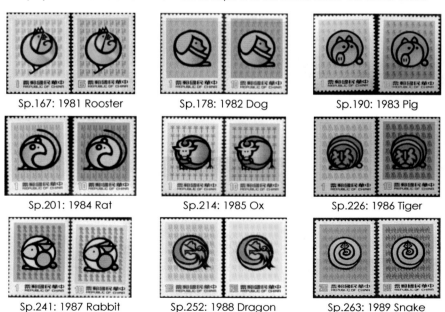

Sp.167: 1981 Rooster   Sp.178: 1982 Dog   Sp.190: 1983 Pig

Sp.201: 1984 Rat   Sp.214: 1985 Ox   Sp.226: 1986 Tiger

Sp.241: 1987 Rabbit   Sp.252: 1988 Dragon   Sp.263: 1989 Snake

Sp.273: 1990 Horse

Sp.287: 1991 Sheep

1992 Monkey

At the end of the cycle, a block of 12 stamps from Rat to Pig was issued (Sp.302 – 1992). Stamps bear the same design with the main issues in the cycle, with an additional Chinese character representing each Zodiac sign on the top left corner of the stamps. Total face value of the block is NT$60 (NT$5 each).

Similarly, there are 12 two-value issues in the third cycle. Each issue also comes with a miniature sheet comprising 4 stamps (two sets with the same design with the individual stamps). The interesting thing about this cycle is that every 3 years there would be a new motif; but all of the stamps are vertical rectangles.

Sp.314: 1993 Rooster

Sp.329: 1994 Dog

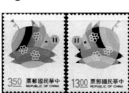

Sp.341: 1995 Pig

Sp.352: 1996 Rat

Sp.364: 1997 Ox

Sp.379: 1998 Tiger

Sp.394: 1999 Rabbit

Sp.407: 2000 Dragon

Sp.418: 2001 Snake

Sp.430: 2002 Horse

Sp.442: 2003 Sheep

Sp.455: 2004 Monkey

The fourth cycle comprises 12 two-value issues. Every 3 years there would be a new motif. Half were issued stamps in vertical rectangles, and half horizontal. Especially, miniature sheets started to have different designs from the main stamp sets.

Sp.472: 2005 Rooster

Sp.482: 2006 Dog

Sp.497: 2007 Pig

Sp.512: 2008 Rat

Sp.526: 2009 Ox

Sp.537: 2010 Tiger

Sp.554: 2011 Rabbit

Sp.566: 2012 Dragon

Sp.581: 2013 Snake

Sp.598: 2014 Horse

Sp.615: 2015 Sheep

Sp.631: 2016 Monkey

The first issue of the fifth cycle, commencing in 2017, again consists of two values and a miniature sheet with different designs. Let's look forward to the rest of the issues!

::: Chinese Literature :::

Journey to the West

Being one of the Four Great Classical Novels of Chinese literature (四大名著), also the very first literature topic to be adapted for PRC stamps, *Journey to West* (西游记) has so many things to offer in modern philately.

The famous fiction was assumed to be created by Wu Cheng'en (吴承恩, c.1500 – 1582) of the Ming dynasty and first published in the 16th century. To date, it has been translated into many languages and has sold millions of copies around the world. The 1986 TV series, being the first media adaption of the novel, still maintains its wide popularity after decades on air, although various new productions have been carried out.

Journey to the West is inspired by a true historical event and character. It depicts Tang dynasty's Buddhist monk Xuanzang (玄奘, c.602 – 664) travelling all the way to India in search for better quality Buddhist scripture.

In the novel, Emperor Taizong of Tang granted him permission to travel to the "Western Region" and obtain the sacred sutras. Three other characters were created as Xuanzang's protectors, who would follow him to help as atonement for their sins in the past.

The first disciple, also one of the most famous and favorite mythological characters all over the world today, is Sun Wukong (孙悟空) - the Monkey King, who used to mess up the entire Heavenly Kingdom and punished by the Buddha with 500-year detainment under the Five Elements Mountain.

The second disciple, known as Zhu Bajie (猪八戒), is a piggy human. He is a Heavenly Marshall in his former life, later being banished for seducing Chang'e - the Goddess of the Moon (嫦娥).

The third disciple is Sha Wujing (沙悟净), also a Heavenly General in his former life. He was punished and banished for destroying the Jade Emperor's valuable vase.

Along the journey, the four pilgrims encountered and defeated various demons, most of whom craved for Xuanzang's flesh to obtain immortality. At the end of the journey, they received enlightenment and forgiveness for their sins.

Journey to the West first appeared on China stamps in 1979 – the famous eight-value issue – T43. Average market price: $90.

Later issues featuring the fiction include 2014-11 (Monkey King Uproar in Heaven), six values.

… China 2015-8, a set of 4 stamps, with a miniature sheet (2015-8M) and a specimen silk miniature sheet. For the later issues, current market value is still less than $5. The silk miniature sheet might cost about $10.

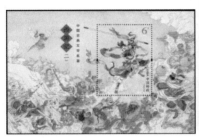

… China 2017-7, another set of 4 stamps, a continuation of the 2015 issue…

More are believed to be released by China Post in the coming years. Do watch out and don't miss out any of them if you already have the other issues in your collection.

Next, let's look at Macau. Only two issues so far. The first is S005 & B006 (2000), a set of 6 stamps in se-tenant block and the miniature sheet. Average price: $15 for both.

… And secondly, S089 & B081 (2007), also a set of 6 stamps in se-tenant block and a miniature sheet… The miniature sheet experienced a dramatic value surge during the 2016 mass speculation. At its peak, some Hong Kong dealers bought back the sheets from Singapore at $60 each, meaning they would sell them at an even higher price to speculators in China. Price has cooled down lately and the current market value fluctuates around $30.

170

Taiwan also has five issues on this theme, each of which has 4 stamps. You can acquire all issues without spending more than $25. The first issue is Sp.377 (1997)…

… Secondly, Sp.480 (2005)…

… Third, Sp.546 (2010)…

… And last but not least, Sp.562 (2011)…

I would suggest the following issue be counted as part of the *Journey to the West* theme: China 2016-24 – Xuanzang. The set is made up of 2 stamps and a miniature sheet, which will cost you less than $5. You can also add the Taiwan stamp of Sp.64 (1970), also featuring Xuanzang, to enrich your collection, although it belongs to another set that is not meant for *Journey for the West*.

That's all for China, Hong Kong, Macau and Taiwan, at least for the time being. But let's extend the topic a little bit further, since many other countries also released stamps that are related to *Journey to the West*.

I would like to briefly introduce to you some of the issues that I find interesting, with the hope to help you shape a much more interesting collection.

First of all, let's look at St. Vincent and the Grenadines' five-value issue featuring Monkey King Uproar in Heaven. The issue also comes with a miniature sheet, and it is part of the 9th Asian Internal Philatelic Exhibition in Beijing in 1996. You may want to collect this set to accompany your T46 and 2014-11. You will spend no more than $10 to acquire the set and the sheet.

For the 33rd Asian Internal Philatelic Exhibition in Guangzhou in 2016, various interesting issues on Monkey King are up for grab. Most dealers will price the stamps at least 3 times of the face value.

Below are a few of them...

Antigua & Barbuda...

Ghana...

Grenada...

Liberia…

Tanzania…

United Nations…

Last but not least, I would like to introduce the latest issue on this topic, coming from the Republic of Mali. It was just issued in 2017, including a sheetlet with 3 stamps, and a miniature sheet with Wu Cheng'en portrait. Looks quite interesting to me!

Again, the price tag would be at least 3 times of the face value.

Romance of the Three Kingdoms

Coming up next, we'll take a look at *Romance of the Three Kingdoms* (三国演义). This famous historical novel is attributed to Luo Guanzhong (罗贯中) – the famous Ming dynasty writer. It is always referred to as one of the Four Great Classical Novels of Chinese literature, along with *Journey to the West*, *Outlaws of the Marsh* and *Dream of the Red Chamber*.

The story focuses on the turbulent years towards the end of the Han dynasty and the division of the kingdom into three rival states that competed for supremacy and total control over China: Wei (魏), Shu (蜀) and Wu (吳).

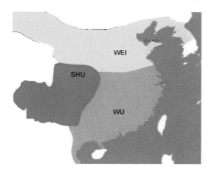

- Wei, or Cao Wei (220 – 265), was founded by Cao Pi (曹丕), son of the renowned Cao Cao (曹操), proclaiming most of the North of China and Northern part of the Korean peninsula.

- Wu, or Eastern Wu (222 – 280), was founded by Sun Quan (孙权), controlling most of the Southern part of modern China, and also Northern part of the modern Vietnam.

- Shu, or Shu Han (221 – 263), was founded by Liu Bei (刘备), a descendant of Emperor Jing of Han. He is usually portrayed as a compassionate and righteous leader, supported by his sworn brothers Guan Yu (关羽) and Zhang Fei (张飞), and the talented military strategist Zhuge Liang (诸葛亮). The kingdom existed on what is now Sichuan province.

The story, part historical, part legend, and part mythical, romanticizes and dramatizes the lives of feudal lords and their retainers. It has a significant impact on Chinese arts and culture; and for us, it provides great inspiration for modern philately!!!

The story has been translated in many languages and sold millions of copies worldwide. It has also been retold in numerous forms including, drama series, comics (Chinese, Japanese and Korean mangas) and video games. Some cardboard strategy games were also derived from the novel, such as Sangokushi Taisen, Generals Order, Portal Three Kingdoms... And now, let's talk about philatelic adaptations.

Romance of the Three Kingdoms first appeared on stamps of Mainland China in 1988. The first issue is indexed as T131, a set of 4 stamps, with a miniature sheet (T131M). Current market value of the set is about $5, and the sheet about $40.

... Secondly, T157 (1990), also consists of 4 stamps. This would cost less than $5.

... Third, 1992-9, also consists of 4 stamps, and also costs less than $5.

... Fourth, 1994-17, a total of 4 stamps and a miniature sheet (1994-17M), each of which would not cost more than $5.

... And finally, 1998-18, also 4 stamps and a miniature sheet (1998-18M). Again, each of them will not cost more than $5.

For Macau, there are two issues. First is S019 & B020 (2001), a set of 4 stamps in se-tenant block and a miniature sheet. The set and the sheet together would cost about $20.

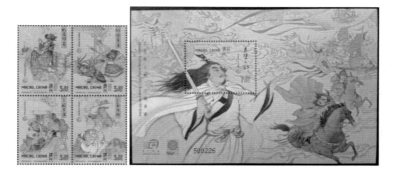

And secondly, S159 & B141 (2013), also a set of 4 stamps in se-tenant block, and a miniature sheet. The set and the sheet together would cost about $20.

Taiwan also issued 4 sets within 10 years, starting with Sp.411 (2000)...

... Followed by Sp.434 (2002)...

... Thirdly, Sp.477 (2005)...

... And finally, Sp.544 (2010)...

You can acquire all four issues without spending more than $20.

I would suggest adding the issues featuring related historical figures into the collection. Hence, China's 2011-23: Lord Guan (Guan Yu), should be considered. This 2-value set and a beautiful miniature sheet (2011-23M) would cost less than $5.

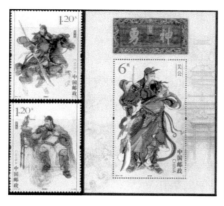

Another set is China's 2014-18: Zhuge Liang. This is also a two-value set with a miniature sheet (2014-18M), also available at less than $5.

Although Guan Yu appeared in Macau's Legends and Myths series and is featured as a God, you can consider include this issue in the collection too. The code is S053 & B047 (2004): God of Guan Di, a set of 4 stamps and a miniature sheet, about $15.

Last but not least, the issue from Republic of Mali (2017), the same series with *Journey to the West* that we've seen earlier. The miniature sheet features Luo Guanzhong.

Outlaws of the Marsh

Outlaws of the Marsh, or *Water Margin* (水浒传) – another zenith of Chinese classical fiction – is considered one of the Four Great Classical Novels. It is attributed to Shi Nai'an (施耐庵, c.1296 – 1372). Based on some real life events, the plot tells stories about a group of 108 outlaw protagonists gathering at Liangshan Marsh during the Song dynasty, under the leadership of Song Jiang, to form a sizable army to resist foreign invaders and suppress rebel forces.

Like other surviving classical works, it has quite a few different editions. It has been translated to many languages, and adapted to many drama series, comics, music and video games. The first translation into Japanese dated back to the 1750s.

The first philately adaption of the fiction was done by China Post in 1987: T123 – a set of 4 stamps (about $5) and a miniature sheet T123M (about $30)…

… Secondly, T138 (1989), a set of 4 stamps, less than $5…

… T167 (1991), also 4 stamps (less than $5) and miniature sheet T167M (less than $10)…

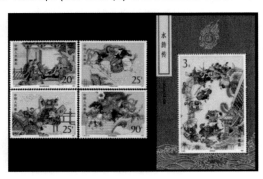

… The fourth issue in the series is 1993-10, a set of 4 stamps, less than $5…

... And 1997-21, 4 values (less than $5) and miniature sheet 1997-21M (less than $10).

Likewise, Macau has 2 issues, both sets of 6 in se-tenant blocks and miniature sheets. The first issue is S041 & B037 (2003), costing about $15...

... Followed by S170 & B150 (2014), also about $15.

Taiwan is in the midst of issuing *Outlaws of the Marsh* stamps. Currently, there are two issues, starting with Sp.570 (2012)...

... Followed by Sp.588 (2013). Each of these sets would be price no more than $5.

As more series would be coming out in the future, do watch out and get your collection up-to-date!

Finally, Republic of Mali's *Water Margin* issue in 2017, a three-value sheetlet and a miniature sheet with the portrait of Shi Nai'an.

Dream of the Red Chamber

Dream of the Red Chamber, or *Dream of the Red Mansions* (红楼梦), is another Great Classical Novel. It was written by Cao Xueqin (曹雪芹, 1715 – 1763) during the 18th century. It also has an alternative name, *The Story of the Stone* (石头记).

The story focuses on the life of the Jia clan's two wealthy houses: The Rongguo House and the Ningguo House. The plot also experiences the clan's declining fortunes and impoverishment. The main character is the carefree adolescent male heir of the family, Jia Baoyu (贾宝玉), who has a special bond with his sickly cousin Lin Daiyu (林黛玉). However, he is predestined to marry another cousin, Xue Baochai (薛宝钗). The plot follows this love triangle against the backdrop of the family's fall from the height of their prestige.

The novel is a precise and detailed observation of the 18th century Chinese society's life and hierarchy. British author and literary critic Anthony West appraised *Dream of the Red Chamber* as one of the great monuments of the world's literature. Though receiving less attention compared to the other three Great Classical Novels, three cinematic adaptations of the fiction have been produced. It has also been adapted to a three-hour opera in English, composed by Bright Sheng and David Henry Hwang. Mei Lanfang also played Lin Daiyu in his famous opera "Daiyu Burying Flowers".

Dream of the Red Chamber was first brought into the philately world in 1981, by China Post, with the renowned T69 issue: Twelve Beauties (with average market value of $70) and a well-sought-after miniature sheet with average market price $250.

Since then China Post did not issue any stamps on this topic until 2014. The first issue was 2014-13, a set of 4 stamps with a miniature sheet (2014-13M).

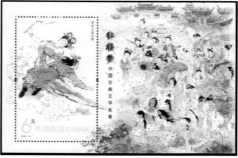

... And subsequently, 2016-15, another set of 4 stamps and a miniature sheet (2016-15M).

Since they are still quite new, they would not cost more than $5 to acquire. More are expected to be issued in the coming years. Don't forget to watch out!

For Macau, there are also 2 issues, each with 6 stamps in se-tenant block and a miniature sheet. The first issue was in 1999 (before Macau was returned to China). Average market price: $15 for both.

... Followed by S027 & B027 (2002). The miniature sheet of this issue was heavily speculated in 2016, and once had it price rocketed to over $60. The price has cooled down by now, about $30 for the set and the sheet together.

Taiwan issued 5 four-value sets, starting with Sp.387 (1998)...

... Followed by Sp.612 (2014)....

... And Sp.620 (2015)...

... Subsequently, Sp.639 (2016)...

... And finally, Sp.654 (2017).

You would be able to source for all five sets at no more than $15 in the market.

For the 9th Asian International Philatelic Exhibition in Beijing in 1996, Grenada & the Grenadines issued a miniature sheet featuring *Dream of the Red Chamber*. It is not very expensive, only a few bucks! So, you should grab it whenever you come across it!

And finally, Republic of Mali's 2017 issue, comprising a three-value sheetlet and a miniature sheet with the portrait of Cao Xueqin. Again, price would be about three times of the face value.

Peony Pavilion

The Peony Pavilion (牡丹亭) is a play written by Tang Xianzu (汤显祖, 1550 – 1616). It is by far the most popular play of the Ming dynasty. The story, set in the final days of the Southern Song dynasty, focuses on the love story of Du Liniang (杜丽娘) and Liu Mengmei (柳梦梅), starting with Du Liniang seeing a stranger (Liu Mengmei) in her dream and fell in love with that young scholar after that, though they'd never met in real life. They met again in Liu's dream after Du Liniang had passed away for obsession and lovesickness. Liu Mengmei tried to exhume her body so that she could be brought back to life. The story ends on a happy note.

T99 (1984) is the Chinese issue featuring this story. It is a four-value set, with a miniature sheet (T99M). Average market price of the set is $8 and the miniature sheet is about $35.

Another set is Macau's S150 & B134 (2012), with 6 values in se-tenant block, and a miniature sheet. These would cost about $25 altogether.

There's another Macau issue featuring the author Tang Xianzu, coming out in 2018. That set can be considered as an accompaniment to this collection.

Romance of the Western Chamber

Romance of the Western Chamber, also known as *Story of the Western Wing* (西厢记) was written by the Yuan dynasty playwright Wang Shifu (王实甫, 1250 – 1337) during the Yuan dysnasty. It is one of the most famous Chinese dramatic works. The plot set during the Tang dynasty, telling the story of a secret love affair between Zhang Junrui (张君瑞), a young scholar, and Cui Yingying (崔莺莺), the daughter of a chief minister of the Tang court. Western wing is the place where the couple often secretly met and consummated their love outside the bond of marriage. Though it has a happy ending, the play has received both appraisal and criticism for its direct attack on the traditional mores and feudal marriage system.

China's T82 (1983) is the first stamp set that features this story. This beautiful set has 4 values, and a miniature sheet (T82M) that is among the most well-sought-after pieces in the T-headed series. Average market price of the set is $40 and the miniature sheet is about $180.

Besides China, Macau also issued a *Romance of the Western Chamber* set in 2005. The set, S066, comprises 6 values in se-tenant block, while the miniature sheet, B059, was also an attractive target for speculation. These would cost about $15 altogether.

187

Bizarre Stories

Bizarre Stories, commonly known as *Liao Zhai*, or *Strange Stories from a Chinese Studio* (聊斋志异) is a collection of almost 500 stories, mainly focusing on ghosts, demons, foxes and immortals in the life of mundane people. The book was written by Qing dynasty writer Pu Songling (蒲松龄, 1640 – 1715). The main purpose of these stories is to implicitly critize the corruption and injustice in the society during his lifetime.

Many of these stories have been adapted for film and television. And finally we have a couple of philatelic issues that illustrate this great literature works.

First thing first, China's 2001-7 issue, the beautiful four-value set with a miniature sheet (2001-7M)...

... Next comes 2002-7, consisting of 4 values in two se-tenant pairs, one vertical and one horizontal.

The third issue, 2003-9, comes in 6 values and a miniature sheet (2003-9M).

These sets should be purchased at no more than $20 altogether.

Macau also came out with Liao Zhai stamps in 2016. The S211 set has 8 values in se-tenant block, and the miniature sheet B179 is also a potential target for speculators.

Others

Literatures

- ✓ Encountering Sorrow (离骚, Li Sao): Macau S052 & B046 (2004)
- ✓ Jin Yong Martial Arts and Chivalry Fictions: Hong Kong 2018
- ✓ Nine Songs (九歌, Jiu Ge): Macau S192 & B165 (2015)
- ✓ The Scholars (儒林外史): China 2011-5

Legends & Folktales

- ✓ Chinese Folktales series: Taiwan Sp.79 (1971), Sp.103 (1974), Sp.114 (1975), Sp.144 (1978), Sp.164 (1980), Sp.188 (1982).
- ✓ Dong Yong and the Seventh Fairy: China 2002-23
- ✓ Gudong: China T51 (1980)
- ✓ Lady White Snake: Taiwan Sp.194 (1983), Macau S113 & B121 (2011), China 2001-26.
- ✓ Liang Shanbo & Zhu Yingtai: Taiwan Sp.236 (1986), Macau S040 & B036 (2003), China 2003-20.
- ✓ Liu Sanjie: China 2012-20.
- ✓ Liu Yi Delivering a Letter: China 2004-14
- ✓ Mulan: China 2002-6, Macau S200 & B170 (2016).
- ✓ The Cowherd & the Weaving Maid: Taiwan Sp.174 (1981), Macau S146 & B133 (2012), China 2010-20.

Chinese Mythology

- ✓ China T120 (1987).
- ✓ Taiwan Sp.317 (1993): The Creation Story.
- ✓ Taiwan Sp.340 (1994): The Invention Story.
- ✓ Taiwan Sp.449 (2003/04): Eight Immortals Crossing the Sea.
- ✓ China 2004-15: Eight Immortals Crossing the Sea.
- ✓ Macau S158 & B140 (2013): Na Tcha.

Chinese Fables

- ✓ China T59 (1981).
- ✓ Taiwan Sp.390 (1998).
- ✓ Taiwan Sp.427 (2001).

Stories of Idioms

- ✓ China 2004-5, 2010-9.
- ✓ Hong Kong 2006, 2011.
- ✓ Macau S014 (2001), S088 & B080 (2007), S111 & B100 (2009).
- ✓ Taiwan Sp.619 (2015), Sp.652 (2017).

Filial Piety Stories

- ✓ Macau S036 & B032 (2002).
- ✓ China 2014-23, 2016-29.

::: Chinese Performing Arts :::

This is another interesting topic, less loaded compared to Zodiac or Literature, but has a mega-costly set within its scope (the Mei Lanfang issue). Rather than that, the rest are quite manageable. Now, let's dive in...

Chinese Operas

China C94 & C94M
The famous Stage Arts of Mei Lanfang set. If you have a tight budget in the beginning, let's not think about this until later.

China T87 (1983)
Female Roles in Beijing Opera: 8 values | Average market price: $45

China 2001-3
Clown Roles in Beijing Opera: 6 values | Average market price: Less than $5

China 2007-5
Acrobatic Male Roles in Beijing Opera: 6 values | Average market price: Less than $5

China 2008-3
Jing Roles in Beijing Opera: 6 values | Average market price: Less than $5

China 2009-29
Stage Arts of Ma Lianliang: 2 values | Average market price: Less than $5

China 2010-14
Kunqu Opera: 3 values | Average market price: Less than $5
Remember *Peony Pavilion*? Check (3-2) out!

<u>China 2017-25</u>
Cantonese Opera: 3 values | Average market price: Less than $5

<u>Hong Kong 1992</u>
Chinese Opera: 4 values | Average market price: Less than $5

<u>Hong Kong 2014</u>
Cantonese Opera: 6 values and a miniature sheet | Less than $10

<u>Hong Kong 2018</u>
Cantonese Opera Repertory: 6 values.

Macau 1991
Chinese Opera: 4 values | Average market value: $15

Macau S216 & B182 (2017)
Chinese Opera – Farewell My Concubine: 4 values in se-tenant block or strip, and a miniature sheet | Average market value: Less than $10

Taiwan Sp.67 (1970)
Chinese Opera: 4 values| Average market value: $15

Taiwan Sp.180 (1982)
Chinese Opera – The Ku Cheng Reunion: 4 values| Average market value: $5

<u>Taiwan Sp.311 (1992)</u>
Chinese Opera: 4 values | Market price: Less than $5

Besides, the China Revolutionary Arts & Opera issues that we've seen earlier can also be added into this theme. However, they are costly. (See earlier for more details)

- ✓ W5: Revolutionary Literature and Art
- ✓ W16: Piano Music from "The Red Lantern"
- ✓ N1-6: Modern Beijing Opera "Taking of the Tiger Mountain"
- ✓ N53-56: Revolutionary Ballet "The White-Haired Girl"

And don't forget about the Guan Hanqing set that we've seen earlier! (C50 & C50M)

Chinese Opera Masks

<u>Taiwan Sp.38 (1966)</u>
Set of 4 values | Average market price: $80

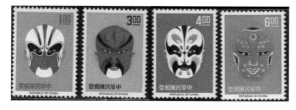

<u>Hong Kong 1974</u>
Art Festivals: Set of 3 values | Average market price: $15
The miniature sheet will cost more (at least double).

<ins>China T45 (1980)</ins>
Set of 8 values | Average market value: $60

<ins>Macau 1998</ins>
Set of 4 values and a miniature sheet | Average price: Less than $5 altogether

Others

✓ China 2014-14: Huangmei Opera
✓ Taiwan Sp.375 (1997): Yuan Opera
✓ Taiwan Sp.401 (1999): Chinese Classical Opera
✓ Taiwan Regional Opera Series: Sp.405 (1999), Sp.429 (2001), Sp.440 (2002)
✓ Taiwan Sp.461 (2004): Yijhen, Taiwanese Folk Art Performance
✓ Macau S132 & B120 (2011): Cantonese Naamyam

::: Chinese Paintings :::

This is a really huge topic I must say! It takes a lot of time and effort to be well-versed in this area. Since the theme can be written into a separate book itself, I will not spend much time here, especially on images. I will just share a comprehensive list of philatelic issues and divide them into sub-themes just for your reference. You may have different views and different ways of classifying them.

I'll highlight some highly sought after sets, with reference market value.

Mainland China

Selected Works by Famous Painters

- ✓ T44 & T44M (1980): Selected Works of *Qi Baishi* – Set of 16 (avg. $150) & miniature sheet (MS – avg. $360)
- ✓ T98 (1984): Selected Works of *Wu Changshuo* – Set of 8
- ✓ 1993-15: Selected Works of *Zheng Banqiao* – Set of 6
- ✓ 1994-14: Selected Works of *Fu Baoshi* – Set of 6
- ✓ 1996-5: Selected Works of *Huang Binhong* – Set of 6
- ✓ 1997-4: Selected Works of *Pan Tianshou* – Set of 6
- ✓ 1998-15: Works of *He Xiangning* – Set of 3
- ✓ 2002-2: Selected Works of *Bada Shanren* – Set of 6
- ✓ 2007-6: Selected Works of *Li Keran* – Set of 6
- ✓ 2009-6: Selected Works of *Shi Tao* – Set of 6 (Se-tenant strip)
- ✓ 2016-3: Selected Works of *Liu Haisu* – Set of 3

Famous Paintings by Ancient Artists

- ✓ T33 (1978): Traditional Silk Paintings of the Warring Period – Set of 2
- ✓ T77 (1982): Fan Paintings of Ming & Qing Dynasties – Set of 6
- ✓ T89 & T89M (1984): Court Ladies Wearing Flowers in Their Hair by *Zhou Fang* – Set of 3 (avg. $15) & MS (avg. $200)
- ✓ T158 (1990): Night Revels of Han Xizai by *Gu Hongzhong* – Set of 5 (Se-tenant strip)
- ✓ 1995-8: Lady Guo's Spring Outing by *Zhang Xuan* – Set of 2 (Se-tenant strip)
- ✓ 2002-5: The Royal Carriage by *Yan Liben* – Set of 1 (MS – avg. $10)
- ✓ 2004-15: Eight Immortals Crossing the Sea – Set of 1 (MS – avg. $8)
- ✓ 2004-26: Along the River during the Qingming Festival by *Zhang Zeduan* – Set of 9 (Sheetlet)
- ✓ 2005-25: Goddess of River Luo by *Gu Kaizhi* – Set of 10 (MS)
- ✓ 2006-29: Magic Horse by an *Anonymous Artist* of Five Dynasties Period – Set of 2 (Se-tenant pair)
- ✓ 2011-25: Eighty Seven Immortals by *Wu Daozi* – Set of 6
- ✓ 2013-8 & 2013-8M: Court Ladies Making Silk by *Emperor Huizong of Song* – Set of 3 (avg. $2) & MS (avg. $5)
- ✓ 2014-4 & 2014-4M: Bathing Horses by *Zhao Mengfu* – Set of 3 (Se-tenant strip) & MS
- ✓ 2015-5 & 2015-5M: Court Ladies Wielding Fans by *Zhou Fang* – Set of 3 (Se-tenant strip – avg. $2) & MS (avg. $4) & silk MS (avg. $15)
- ✓ 2016-5 & 2015-5M: Hermit Arts by *Sun Li* – Set of 3 (Se-tenant strip) & MS
- ✓ 2017-3: One Thousand Li of Rivers and Mountains by *Wang Ximeng* – Set of 9 (Sheetlet)

Specialties

- ✓ T28 & T28M (1978): Galloping Horse Paintings – Set of 10 (avg. $80) & MS (avg. $680)
- ✓ J60 (1980): UNESCO's Exhibition of Chinese Paintings – Set of 3
- ✓ T141 (1989): Contemporary Chinese Art – Set of 3
- ✓ 2010-25: Plum Blossom, Orchid, Bamboo & Chrysanthemums – Set of 4
- ✓ 2015-4: The 24 Solar Terms (I) – Set of 6 (MS)
- ✓ 2016-10: The 24 Solar Terms (II) – Set of 6 (MS)
- ✓ 2017-6: Four Seasons – Set of 4

Besides, quite a number of issues on scenery (mountains, rivers etc.) can also be counted as part of the painting theme.

Taiwan

Famous Paintings by Ancient Artists

- ✓ Sp.16 (1960): Ancient Chinese Paintings from the National Palace Museum – Set of 4
- ✓ Sp.27 (1962): Ancient Chinese Paintings from the National Palace Museum – Set of 4 (The famous 4 Emperors issue) | avg. $500
- ✓ Sp.39 (1966): Ancient Chinese Paintings from the National Palace Museum – Set of 4
- ✓ Sp.53 (1968): A City of Cathay by *Zhang Zeduan* – Set of 5 (Se-tenant pair of 2 + 2)
- ✓ Sp.84 (1972): The Emperor's Procession Departing from the Palace – Set of 8 (Se-tenant strip of 5 + 3) | avg. $35
- ✓ Sp.85 (1972): The Emperor's Procession Returning to the Palace – Set of 8 (Se-tenant strip of 5 + 3) | avg. $35
- ✓ Sp.94 (1973): Spring Morning in Han Palace by *Qiu Ying*– Set of 14 (2 Se-tenant strips of 5 + 4) | avg. $40
- ✓ Sp.109 (1974): Festivals for the New Year by *Ding Guanpeng* – Set of 8 (Se-tenant strip of 5 + 3)
- ✓ Sp.150 (1979): Children Playing Games on Winter Day by *Su Hanchen* – Set of 4 (Se-tenant block) & MS
- ✓ Sp.166 (1980): Landscape Paintings by *Qiu Ying* – Set of 4 (Se-tenant block & MS)
- ✓ Sp.177 (1981): One Hundred Young Boys – Set of 10 (Se-tenant block) | avg. $25
- ✓ Sp.189 (1982): Lohan Paintings by *Liu Songnian* – Set of 3 & MS
- ✓ Sp.207 (1984): Famous Paintings by *Zhang Daqian* – Set of 3
- ✓ Sp.210 (1985): Ancient Paintings by an *Anonymous Song Painters* – Set of 4
- ✓ Sp.227 (1986): Hermit Anglers on a Mountain Stream by *Tang Yin* – Set of 5 (Se-tenant strip)
- ✓ Sp.232 (1986): Famous Paintings by *Pu Xinru* – Set of 3
- ✓ Sp.250 (1987): Red Cliff in Zhao Bosu's Style by *Wen Zhengming* – Set of 10 (Se-tenant block)
- ✓ Sp.261 (1988): Ancient Chinese Paintings by *Shen Zhou* – Set of 4 (Se-tenant block)
- ✓ Sp.298 (1991): Ancient Chinese Paintings by *Giuseppe Castiglione* (*Lang Shining*) – Set of 3
- ✓ Sp.310 (1992): Silk Tapestry of National Palace Museum – Set of 2 & MS
- ✓ Sp.344 (1995): Court Ladies on Horseback by *Li Gonglin* –Set of 4 (Se-tenant strip) & MS
- ✓ Sp.354 (1996): Forest Grotto at Juqu by *Wang Meng* – Set of 4 (Se-tenant block)
- ✓ Sp.382 (1998): Kublai Khan's Hunting by *Liu Guandao*
- ✓ Sp.397 (1999): Joy in Peacetime Paintings – Set of 4 & MS
- ✓ Sp.466 (2004): Listening to the Lute by *Li Song* – Set of 2 (MS)
- ✓ Sp.508 (2007): Eighteen Scholars of the Tang by *Emperor Huizong of Song* – Set of 10 (Se-tenant block)
- ✓ Sp.523 (2008): A Hundred Deers by *Ignatius Sichelbart* – Set of 10 (MS)
- ✓ Sp.549 (2010): Nine Elders of Mount Xiang (I) – Set of 3 (MS)
- ✓ Sp.564 (2011): Nine Elders of Mount Xiang (II) – Set of 3 (Sheetlet)
- ✓ Sp.604 (2014): Children at Play – Set of 5
- ✓ Sp.629 (2015): Ancient Chinese Paintings by *Giuseppe Castiglione* (*Lang Shining*) – Set of 4 (avg. $3) & silk MS (avg. $6)
- ✓ Sp.637 (2016): Ancient Chinese Paintings from the National Palace Museum – Set of 3

Specialties

- ✓ Sp.60 (1969): Flowers and Birds Paintings – Set of 4
- ✓ Sp.72 (1970): Occupations of 12 Months – Set of 12
- ✓ Sp.80 (1971): The Ten Prized Dogs Paintings – Set of 10 (avg. $60)
- ✓ Sp.95 (1973): Chinese Famous Paintings on Folding Fans – Set of 4
- ✓ Sp.97 (1973): The Eight Prized Horses – Set of 8 (avg. $40) & MS (avg. $60)
- ✓ Sp.104 (1974): Famous Paintings on Moon-shaped Fans – Set of 4
- ✓ Sp.111 (1975): Chinese Famous Paintings on Folding Fans – Set of 4
- ✓ Sp.113 (1975): Ancient Chinese Figures – Set of 4

- ✓ Sp.115 (1975): Famous Paintings on Moon-shaped Fans – Set of 4
- ✓ Sp.124 (1976): Famous Paintings on Moon-shaped Fans – Set of 4
- ✓ Sp.127 (1977): Pine, Bamboo, Plum Three Friends of Winter – Set of 3
- ✓ Sp.157 (1979): Pine and Bamboo Paintings – Set of 4
- ✓ Sp.185 (1982): Classical Tang Poetry – Set of 4 (avg. $20)
- ✓ Sp.192 (1983): Classical Song Poetry – Set of 4 (avg. $18)
- ✓ Sp.204 (1984): Classical Yuan Poetry – Set of 4 (avg. $25)
- ✓ Sp.218 (1985): Chinese Classical Poetry, Confucius' "Book of Odes" – Set of 4 (avg. $15)
- ✓ Sp.279 (1990): Classical Yuefu – Set of 4
- ✓ Sp.308 (1992): Classical Gushi – Set of 4
- ✓ Def.112 (1995): Ancient Chinese Engraving Art – Set of 15
- ✓ Sp.378 (1997): National Palace Museum's Bird Manual – Set of 20 (Se-tenant block)
- ✓ Sp.385 (1998): Zhong Kui Paintings – Set of 2
- ✓ Def.115 (1998): Ancient Chinese Engraving Art – Set of 4
- ✓ Def.115 (1999): Ancient Chinese Engraving Art – Set of 9
- ✓ Def.115 (2000): Ancient Chinese Engraving Art – Set of 2
- ✓ Sp.406 (1999): National Palace Museum's Bird Manual – Set of 4
- ✓ Sp.417 (2000): National Palace Museum's Bird Manual – Set of 4
- ✓ Sp.428 (2001): National Palace Museum's Bird Manual – Set of 4
- ✓ Sp.439 (2002): National Palace Museum's Bird Manual – Set of 4
- ✓ Sp.542 (2003): National Palace Museum's Bird Manual – Set of 4
- ✓ Sp.490 (2006): Song Dynasty's Calligraphy & Paintings – Set of 4 & MS
- ✓ Sp.580 (2012): Three Friends and a Hundred Birds – Set of 3 (Sheetlet) & MS
- ✓ Sp.663 (2016): Painting and Calligraphy on the Fan (I) – Set of 2 MS
- ✓ Sp.635 (2016): Immortal Blossoms of an Eternal Spring (I) – Set of 8
- ✓ Sp.647 (2016): Painting and Calligraphy on the Fan (II) – Set of 2 MS
- ✓ Sp.635 (2017): Immortal Blossoms of an Eternal Spring (II) – Set of 8

Madame Chiang Kai-shek's Landscape Paintings

- ✓ Sp.117 (1975): Madame Chiang Kai-shek's Landscape Paintings – Set of 4
- ✓ Sp.130 (1977): Madame Chiang Kai-shek's Landscape Paintings – Set of 4
- ✓ Sp.246 (1987): *Madame Chiang Kai-shek*'s Landscape Paintings – Set of 4

Modern Paintings

- ✓ Sp.443 (2002): Modern Taiwanese Paintings – Set of 4
- ✓ Sp.454 (2003): Modern Taiwanese Paintings – Set of 4
- ✓ Sp.459 (2004): Modern Taiwanese Paintings – Set of 4
- ✓ Sp.534 (2009): Modern Taiwanese Paintings – Set of 3 (Se-tenant block)
- ✓ Sp.548 (2010): Modern Taiwanese Paintings – Set of 2
- ✓ Sp.656 (2017): Modern Ink-Wash Paintings – Set of 4

Hong Kong

- ✓ 2009: Hong Kong Museum Collection
- ✓ 2014: Hong Kong Museums Collection – Modern Paintings by *Mr. Wu Guanzhong*
- ✓ 2017: Paintings and Calligraphy of *Professor Jao Tsung-i*

Macau

- ✓ 1985: 25th Anniversary of Luís de Camões Museum
- ✓ S162 & B144 (2013): Chinese Calligraphy & Paintings
- ✓ S206 & B174 (2016): Paintings of Macau's Famous Artists
- ✓ S208 & B176 (2016): Chinese Landscape Paintings

::: Famous People :::

Here comes a very exciting theme. There are thousands of China stamps featuring people that you can collect. Some of them are very expensive, and some quite affordable. Depending on what you want, who you admire or who you would like to be present in your stamp album, you'll build the collection around your scope of focus.

In this section, I will share with you how I classify and collect stamps in this topic.

Dr. Sun Yat-sen

Dr. Sun Yat-sen is among the first figures that appeared on China stamps. His presence covers almost all areas of Chinese philately, from Chinese Republic, Japanese Occupation, Chinese Communist Liberated Areas, PRC, Hong Kong, Macau and Taiwan. Hence, collecting stamps on Dr. Sun Yat-sen can take a lot of time and effort, and of course money.

Let's take a closer look at the issues related to the Father of Modern China!

1st issue (1931-37)	2nd issue (1931-37)	3rd issue (1938-41)

4th issue   5th issue

3rd issue Redrawn (1942-45)   6th issue (1944-46)   2nd issue Redrawn (1944-46)   7th issue (1945-46)   8th issue (1945-46)

9th issue (1946-47)   10th issue (1947)   11th issue (1947-48)   12th issue (1948)   13th issue (1949)

14th issue (1949)   Northeast China (1946-49)   Formosa 1st issue (1947)   Formosa 2nd issue (1948)

<u>Chinese Republic</u>

- ✓ Com.3 (1912): National Revolution Commemorative
- ✓ Com.9 (1929): Dr. Sun Yat-sen's State Burial (General issue & Restricted issues)
- ✓ 1944: 50th Anniversary of the Chinese Kuomintang
- ✓ 1945: 20th Death Anniversary of Dr. Sun Yat-sen
- ✓ Definitive issues between 1931 and 1949: 14 issues and 3 local issues for Northeast and Formosa (Taiwan)
- ✓ Surcharge issues and Provincial restricted issues
- ✓ Japanese occupation overprint issues

I am not a fan of surcharge stamps. So, I will not collect those personally. But I've seen people who are really specialized in surcharge and overprints, and that takes them much more time than what they spend on any other specializations.

So, if you collect Dr. Sun Yat-sen of this period, it is up to you to focus on non-surcharge or surcharge issues, or both if your capacity allows.

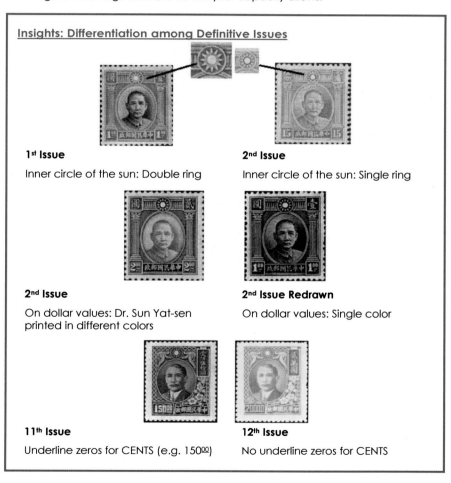

Insights: Differentiation among Definitive Issues

1st Issue

Inner circle of the sun: Double ring

2nd Issue

Inner circle of the sun: Single ring

2nd Issue

On dollar values: Dr. Sun Yat-sen printed in different colors

2nd Issue Redrawn

On dollar values: Single color

11th Issue

Underline zeros for CENTS (e.g. 150⁰⁰)

12th Issue

No underline zeros for CENTS

13th Issue	14th Issue
Underline zeros for CENTS (e.g. 1000⁰⁰). No cents values. All are dollar values.	All are cent values. No dollar values.

Formosa 1st Issue	Formosa 2nd Issue
Underline zeros for CENTS (e.g. 1⁰⁰)	No underline zeros for CENTS

Liberated Areas

- ✓ Surcharge issues

Mainland China

- ✓ Early PRC surcharge issues
- ✓ C38 (1956): 90th Birth Anniversary of Dr. Sun Yat-sen
- ✓ C90 (1961): 50th Anniversary of Xinhai Revolution
- ✓ C120 (1966): Birth Centenary of Dr. Sun Yat-sen
- ✓ J68 (1980): 70th Anniversary of Xinhai Revolution
- ✓ J132 (1986): Celebrated Leaders of the Xinhai Revolution
- ✓ J133 (1986): 120th Birth Anniversary of Dr. Sun Yat-sen
- ✓ 2006-28: 140th Birth Anniversary of Dr. Sun Yat-sen
- ✓ 2016-32: 150th Birth Anniversary of Dr. Sun Yat-sen
- ✓ 2011-23: Centenary of Xinhai Revolution

Hong Kong

- ✓ 2006: 140th Birth Anniversary of Dr. Sun Yat-sen
- ✓ 2011: Centenary of Xinhai Revolution
- ✓ 2016: 150th Birth Anniversary of Dr. Sun Yat-sen

Macau

- ✓ 1986: 120th Birth Anniversary of Dr. Sun Yat-sen
- ✓ S137 & B124 (2011): Centenary of Xinhai Revolution
- ✓ S138 & B125 (2011): 140th Anniversary of Kiang Wu Hospital Charitable Association
- ✓ S209 & B177 (2016): 150th Birth Anniversary of Dr. Sun Yat-sen

Taiwan

- ✓ Sp.74 (1959): Leaders of Democracy
- ✓ Com.72 (1961): 50th National Day of ROC

- ✓ Com.91 (1963): 10th Anniversary of Adoption of Land-to-Tillers Program
- ✓ Com.101 (1964): 70th Anniversary of Kuomintang
- ✓ Com.107 (1965): Birth Centenary of Dr. Sun Yat-sen
- ✓ Sp.110 (1975): Dr. Sun Yat-sen Memorial Hall
- ✓ Com.161 (1976): 11th National Congress of the Kuomintang
- ✓ Com.183 (1981): 70th Anniversary of the ROC
- ✓ Com.212 (1985): 120th Birth Anniversary of Dr. Sun Yat-sen
- ✓ Com.249 (1994): 100th Anniversary of Kuomintang
- ✓ Com.320 (2011): Centenary of the ROC
- ✓ Com.330 (2015): 150th Birth Anniversary of Dr. Sun Yat-sen

To add into this theme, I recommend you to look for issues of other countries to accompany with your Chinese Sun Yat-sen stamps. Some examples as follows:

- ✓ 1945 US: China Resistance in WWII (Dr. Sun Yat-sen & President Lincoln)
- ✓ 1961 US: 50th Anniversary of the ROC
- ✓ 1965 USSR: Birth Centenary of Dr. Sun Yat-sen
- ✓ 1966 Argentina: Birth Centenary of Dr. Sun Yat-sen
- ✓ 1986 USSR: 120th Birth Anniversary of Dr. Sun Yat-sen
- ✓ 1997 Guyana: 75th Death Anniversary of Dr. Sun Yat-sen
- ✓ 2016 Philippines: 150th Birth Anniversary of Dr. Sun Yat-sen

Chairman Mao Zedong

As the founding father of the People's Republic of China, Mao Zedong is praised by most people living in Mainland, and appeared on many stamps of Chinese Liberated Areas and PRC.

Below is the list of issues that directly or indirectly feature Chairman Mao.

Liberated Areas – Refer to the earlier section of this chapter.

Mainland China (PRC)

- ✓ C2 & C2NE (1950): Chinese People's Political Consultative Conference
- ✓ C4 & C4NE (1950): Inauguration of the People's Republic of China
- ✓ C9 (1951): 30th Anniversary of the Communist Party of China
- ✓ C71 (1959): 10th Anniversary of the People's Republic of China
- ✓ C74 (1960): 25th Anniversary of the Zunyi Meeting
- ✓ C109 (1965): 30th Anniversary of the Zunyi Meeting
- ✓ C115 (1965): 20th Anniversary of the Victory of the Sino-Japanese War
- ✓ W1 (1967): Thoughts of Chairman Mao (I)
- ✓ W2 (1967): Long Live Chairman Mao
- ✓ W4 (1967): Anniversary of the Chinese Communist Party
- ✓ W6 (1967): 18th Anniversary of the People's Republic
- ✓ W7 (1967-68): Poems of Chairman Mao
- ✓ W9 (1968): Chairman Mao's Anti-American Declaration
- ✓ W10 (1968): Directives of Chairman Mao
- ✓ W12 (1968): Chairman Mao en route to Anyuan
- ✓ W13 (1968): Thoughts of Chairman Mao (II)
- ✓ J21 (1977): 1st Death Anniversary of Chairman Mao
- ✓ J22 (1977): Chairman Mao Memorial Hall
- ✓ J97 (1983): 90th Birth Anniversary of the Comrade Mao Zedong
- ✓ 1993-17 & 1993-7M: Birth Centenary of Comrade Mao Zedong
- ✓ 1999-13: 50th Anniversary of the People's Political Consultative Conference
- ✓ 2003-25: 110th Birth Anniversary of Comrade Mao Zedong
- ✓ 2013-30: 120th Birth Anniversary of Comrade Mao Zedong

President Chiang Kai-shek

Being the leader of the Republic of China for almost half a decade, from 1928 until his death in 1975, President Chiang Kai-shek shared the ups and downs of the regime and also appeared on many stamps of the Republic of China during both periods.

Chinese Republic

- ✓ Com.8 (1929): Commemoration of National Unification (General issue & Restricted issues)
- ✓ 1944: Sino-American and Anglo-Chinese Equal Treaty
- ✓ 1945: Commemoration of Inauguration
- ✓ 1945: Victory Commemoration
- ✓ 1946: President Chiang's 60th Birthday (General issue & Restricted issues)

Taiwan

- ✓ Com.35 (1952): 2nd Anniversary of Chiang Kai-shek's Re-election as President
- ✓ Com.36 (1953): 3rd Anniversary of Chiang Kai-shek's Re-election as President
- ✓ Def.80 (1953): President Chiang Kai-shek
- ✓ Com.42 (1955): 1st Anniversary of President Chiang Kai-shek's second Term Inauguration
- ✓ Sp.4 (1955): President Chiang Kai-shek
- ✓ Com.50 (1956): President Chiang's 70th Birthday
- ✓ Sp.8 (1958): President Chiang Kai-shek
- ✓ Com.70 (1961): 1st Anniversary of President Chiang Kai-shek's third Term Inauguration
- ✓ Com.72 (1961): 50th National Day of ROC
- ✓ Sp.42 (1966): President Chiang Kai-shek
- ✓ Com.111 (1967): 1st Anniversary of President Chiang Kai-shek's fourth Term Inauguration
- ✓ Com.123 (1968): President Chiang's Meritorious Services
- ✓ Com.158 (1976): 1st Anniversary of the Death of President Chiang Kai-shek
- ✓ Com.160 (1976): President Chiang's 90th Birthday
- ✓ Com.161 (1976): 11th National Congress of the Kuomintang
- ✓ Com.168 (1978): 3rd Death Anniversary of President Chiang Kai-shek
- ✓ Com.177 (1980): 5th Death Anniversary of President Chiang Kai-shek
- ✓ Com.183 (1981): 70th Anniversary of the ROC
- ✓ Com.207 (1985): 10th Death Anniversary of President Chiang Kai-shek
- ✓ Com.210 (1985): 40th Anniversary of Victory in the Sino-Japanese War & Taiwan Retrocession
- ✓ Com.217 (1986): President Chiang's 100th Birthday

Individuals

Besides Dr. Sun Yat Sen, Chairman Mao Zedong & President Chiang Kai-shek, below is the list of people featured on individual stamps or sets in the realm of Chinese philately. For the convenience of looking up, I summarize the list below in alphabetical order. The list will definitely get longer as time goes by. Some of the issues might overlap other topics that we have discussed earlier on in this book.

A

- ✓ **Abraham Lincoln** (*US president*): Taiwan Sp.12 (159)
- ✓ **Albert Einstein** (*American physicist*): China J36 (1979), Taiwan Com.302 (2005)
- ✓ **António Ramalho Eanes** (*President of Portugal*): Macau 1985

B

- ✓ **Bao Zheng** (Lord Bao, *Song dynasty official*): China 2015-16 & 2015-16M
- ✓ **Belchior Carneiro** (Bishop, *Portuguese missionary*): Macau 1969
- ✓ **Benjamin Franklin** (*US politician*): US Postal Agencies in Shanghai 1919
- ✓ **Bo Yibo** (*Chinese Communist military & political leader*): China 2009-3

C

- ✓ **Cai Yuanpei** (*Chinese educator*): Taiwan Sp.43 (1967), China J145 (1988)
- ✓ **Cao Chong** (*Eastern Han warlord*): China 2008-13
- ✓ **Carlos I** (*King of Portugal*): Macau1894, 1898-1900, 1900, 1902, 1903
- ✓ **Chen Cheng** (Chinese politician & military leader)**:** Taiwan C.115 (1968)
- ✓ **Chen Jiageng** (Tan Kah Kee, *Chinese businessman & philanthropist*): China J106 (1984)
- ✓ **Chen Tianhua** (*Chinese revolutionary*): Taiwan Sp.229 (1986)
- ✓ **Chen Yi** (*Chinese military commander & politician*): China J181 (1991)
- ✓ **Chen Yun** (*Chinese politician*): China 2000-12
- ✓ **Chiang Ching-kuo** (*Taiwan President*): Taiwan Com.229 (1989), Com.266 (1998), Com.313 (2009)
- ✓ **Chiang Wei-shui** (*Taiwanese politician*): Taiwan Sp.507 (2007)
- ✓ **Clara Zetkin** (*German Marxist theorist & activist*): China C76 (1960), J53 (1980)
- ✓ **Confucius** (*Ancient Chinese philosopher*): Chinese Republic 1947, Taiwan Com.223 (1987), China J162 & J162M (1989), 2010-22 & 2010-22M

D

- ✓ **Dai Chuanxian** (*ROC journalist*): Taiwan Com.228 (1989)
- ✓ **Deng Xiaoping** (*Chinese politician*): China 1997-10 & 1997-10M, 1998-3, 1998-30, 1999-18 & 1999-18M, 2000-S1, 2004-17 & 2004-17M, 2014-17, Hong Kong 2004, Macau S055 & B048 (2004)
- ✓ **Deng Yingchao** (*Chinese politician*): China 2004-3
- ✓ **Dong Biwu** (*Chinese Communist political leader*): China J123 (1986)
- ✓ **Du Fu** (*Tang dynasty poet*): China C93 (1962)
- ✓ **D.S. Kotnis** (*Indian physician*): China J83 (1982)

E

- ✓ **Edward VII** (*King of the UK*): Hong Kong 1903, 1904-1906, 1907-1911
- ✓ **Eleanor Roosevelt** (*American politician*): Taiwan C.102 (1964)
- ✓ **Enver Hoxha** (*Albanian Communist leader*): China C108 (1964), N25-28
- ✓ **Elizabeth** (*British Queen Mother*): Hong Kong 1980, 1985
- ✓ **Elizabeth II** (*Queen of the UK*): Hong Kong 1953 (Coronation), 1954-1962, 1962-1973, 1972 (Silver Wedding), 1973, 1975-1982, 1975 (Royal Visit), 1977 (Silver Jubilee), 1978 (Coronation Anniversary), 1982, 1986 (Birthday), 1987, 1987-1988, 1992 (Accession), 1992 (Machin), 1993-1997 (Machin)

F

- ✓ **Fan Zhongyan** (*Song dynasty politician & educator*): Taiwan Com.231 (1989)
- ✓ **Fang Zhimin** (*Chinese Communist military & political leader*): China 1999-8
- ✓ **Freidrich Engels** (*German philosopher*): China C35 (1955) & C80 (1960)

G

- ✓ **Gago Coutino** (*Portuguese naval officer*): Macau 1969
- ✓ **George Chinnery** (*English painter*): Macau 1974
- ✓ **George V** (*King of the UK*): Hong Kong 1912-1921, 1921-1937, 1935 (Silver Jubilee)
- ✓ **George VI** (*King of the UK*): Hong Kong 1937 (Coronation), 1938-1952, 1946 (Victory), 1948 (Silver Wedding)
- ✓ **George Washington** (*US president*): US Postal Agencies in Shanghai 1919
- ✓ **Guan Hanqing** (*Yuan dynasty playwright*): China C50 & C50M (1958)
- ✓ **Guan Yu** (Lord Guan, *General of the Three Kingdoms period*): China 2011-23 & 2011-23M, Macau S053 & B047 (2004)
- ✓ **Guo Moruo** (*Chinese author & politician*): China J87 (1982)

H

- ✓ **He Long** (*Chinese Communist military leader*): China J126 (1986)
- ✓ **Henry the Navigator** (*Prince of Portugal*): Macau 1994
- ✓ **Hu Shih** (*Chinese philosopher & diplomat*): Taiwan Com.234 (1990)
- ✓ **Hua Tuo** (*Eastern Han dynasty physician*): Taiwan Sp.65 (1970)

J

- ✓ **James Legge** (*Scottish sinologist & missionary*): Hong Kong 1994
- ✓ **Jiao Yulu** (*Chinese politician*): China 1992-15
- ✓ **Jingu** (*Japanese Empress*): Japanese Post Offices in China 1908-1914

✓ **Johann Adam Schall von Bell** (*German revolutionary*): Taiwan Com.238 (1992)
✓ **Joseph Stalin** (*Russian Communist leader*): Liberated Areas, China C27 (1954), J49 (1979)

K

✓ **Karl Marx** (*German philosopher*): China C22 (1953), C46 (1958), C98 (1963), J90 (1983)
✓ **Kong Rong** (*Eastern Han official*): China 2007-14

L

✓ **Lei Feng** (*Chinese Communist soldier*): China J26 (1978), 2013-3
✓ **Li Dazhao** (*Co-founder of the Chinese Communist Party*): China J164 (1989)
✓ **Li Fuchun** (*Chinese politician*): China J168 (1990)
✓ **Li Lisan** (*Chinese Communist leader*): China 1999-17
✓ **Li Weihan** (*Chinese politician*): China J127 (1986)
✓ **Li Xiannian** (*Chinese politician*): China 2009-12
✓ **Liao Chengzhi** (*Chinese politician*): China J153 (1988)
✓ **Liao Zhongkai** (*Chinese Kuomintang leader*): China J137 (1987)
✓ **Lin Boqu** (*Chinese politician*): China J124 (1986)
✓ **Lin Juemin** (*Chinese revolutionary*): Taiwan Sp.206 (1984)
✓ **Lin Sen** (*Chinese politician*): Chinese Republic 1945, Taiwan Com.110 (1966)
✓ **Lin Yutang** (*Chinese writer*): Taiwan Com.247 (1994)
✓ **Lin Zexu** (*Qing dynasty official*): China J115 (1985), Taiwan Sp.93 (1973), Macau S174 & B153 (2014)
✓ **Liu Shaoqi** (*Chinese politician*): China J96 (1983), 1998-25
✓ **Liu Yingchun** (*Chinese Communist soldier*): China C123 (1967)
✓ **Louis Braille** (*French educator & inventor of Braille system*): Macau S106 (2009)
✓ **Louis Pasteur** (*French chemist & microbiologist*): Taiwan Com.253 (1995)
✓ **Lu Haodong** (*Chinese revolutionary*): Taiwan Sp.151 (1979)
✓ **Lu Xun** (*Chinese writer*): China C11 (1951), C91 (1962), J11 (1976), J67 (1981)
✓ **Luis** (*King of Portugal*): Macau 1888
✓ **Luís de Camões** (*Portuguese poet*): Macau 1979
✓ **Luo Fuxing** (*Chinese revolutinary*): Taiwan Com.206 (1985)
✓ **Luo Ronghuan** (*Chinese Communist military leader*): China 1992-17

M

✓ **Ma Lianliang** (*Beijing opera singer*): China 2009-29
✓ **Manuel das Nóbrega** (*Portuguese priest*): Macau 1954
✓ **Mao Dun** (*Chinese novelist & politician*): China J129 (1986)
✓ **Matteo Ricci** (*Italian missionary*): Taiwan Com.192 (1983)
✓ **Mei Lanfang** (*Beijing opera singer*): China C94 & C94M (1962)

N

✓ **Ni Yingdian** (*Chinese revolutionary*): Taiwan Sp.264 (1989)
✓ **Nie Er** (*PRC anthem composer*): China J57 (1982)
✓ **Nie Rongzhen** (*Chinese Communist military leader*): China 1999-19
✓ **Norman Bethune** (*Canadian physician*): China C84 (1960), J50 (1979), J166 (1990)

O

✓ **Óscar Carmona** (*Marshal, Portuguese politician*): Macau 1970

P

✓ **Paul Yu Pin** (*Chinese Cardinal*): Taiwan Com.286 (2001)
✓ **Pedro Cabral** (*Portuguese explorer*): Macau 1968
✓ **Peng Dehuai** (*Chinese Communist military leader*): China J155 (1988)
✓ **Peng Zhen** (*Chinese politician*): China 2002-24
✓ **Puyi** (*Chinese Emperor*): Manchukuo 1932, 1934

Q

✓ **Qi Jiguang** (*Ming dynasty military general*): China 2008-17
✓ **Qian Mu** (*Ch'ien Mu, Chinese philosopher*): Taiwan Com.246 (1994)
✓ **Qiu Fengjia** (*Taiwanese patriot*): Taiwan Sp.96 (1973)
✓ **Qiu Jin** (*Chinese writer*): Taiwan Sp.46 (1967)
✓ **Qu Qiubai** (*Chinese Communist leader*): China J157 (1989)

R

✓ **Rebelo da Silva** (*Portuguese novelist*): Macau 1969
✓ **Ren Bishi** (*Chinese Communist military & political leader*): China J100 & J101 (1984)
✓ **Robert Baden-Powell** (*British Lieutenant General*): Hong Kong 2007, Macau S090 & B082 (2007)
✓ **Robert Hart** (*British diplomat & Qing dynasty official*): Taiwan Com.2015 (1985)
✓ **Robert Koch** (*German physician & microbiologist*): China J74 (1982)
✓ **Robert Morrison** (*Anglo Scottish missionary*): Macau S091 (2007)
✓ **Rowland Hill** (*British teacher & inventor of the world's first postage stamp*): Taiwan Com.174 (1979), Macau 1990

S

✓ **Sebastião José de Carvalho e Melo** (Marquis de Pombal, Portuguese *statesman*): Macau 1925
✓ **Shi Xianru** (*Chinese revolutionary*): Taiwan Sp.160 (1980)
✓ **Sima Guang** (Song dynasty historian): China 2004-11
✓ **Song Ci** (*Song dynasty physician*): China 2016-7
✓ **Song Meiling** (*Madam Chiang Kai-shek*): Taiwan Com.68 (1961), Sp.33 (1965), Sp.595 (2013)
✓ **Song Qingling** (*Madam Sun Yat-sen*): China J82 (1982), 1993-2
✓ **Song Renqiong** (*Chinese Communist general*): China 2010-2
✓ **Sun Tzu** (Sun Zi, *ancient Chinese military strategist*): China 1995-26

T

✓ **Tan Yankai** (*Chinese politician*): Chinese Republic Com.11 (1933)
✓ **Tao Zhu** (*Chinese politician*): China J146 (1988)
✓ **Tao Xingzhi** (*Chinese educator & reformer*): China J183 (1991)
✓ **Teresa Teng** (*Taiwanese singer*): Taiwan Sp.621 (2015)

U

✓ **Ulanhu** (*Chinese politician*): China 2006-31

V

✓ **Victoria** (*Queen of the UK*): Hong Kong 1862-1863, 1863-1871, 1876-1877, 1880, 1882-1886, 1885, 1891, 1898, 1900-1901
✓ **Victor Emmanuel III** (*King of Italy*): Italian Post Offices in China 1917-1921
✓ **Visconde de São Januário** (*Portuguese diplomat*): Macau 1974
✓ **V.I. Lenin** (*Russian Communist leader*): Liberated Areas, China C26 (1954), C34 (1955), C77 (1960), C111 (1965), J57 (1980)

W

✓ **Wang Jiaxiang** (*Chinese Communist leader*): China J130 (1986)
✓ **Wang Jinxi** (*Chinese model worker*): China N44 (1972)
✓ **Wang Yunwu** (*Chinese politician & scholar*): Taiwan Com.222 (1987)
✓ **Wang Zhaojun** (*One of the Four Beauties of Ancient China*): China 1994-10 & 1994-10M
✓ **Wei Guoqing** (*Chinese Communist military leader*): China 2013-20
✓ **Wen Yanbo** (*Song dynasty official*): China 2010-12
✓ **Wu Yue** (*Chinese revolutionary*): Taiwan Sp.245 (1987)
✓ **Wu Zhihui** (*Chinese linguist & philosopher*): Taiwan Com.93 (1964), Com.193 (1983)

X

✓ **Xi Zhongxun** (*Chinese Communist leader*): China 2013-27
✓ **Xian Xinghai** (Sinn Sing Hoi, *Chinese composer*): China J111 (1985)
✓ **Xiong Chengji** (*Chinese revolutionary*): Taiwan Sp.291 (1991)
✓ **Xu Beihong** (*Chinese painter*): China J114 (1985)
✓ **Xu Guangqi** (*Ming dynasty scientist*): Taiwan Com.100 (1964)
✓ **Xu Xiake** (*Ming dynasty geographer*): China J136 (1987)
✓ **Xu Xiangqian** (*Chinese military leader*): China J184 (1991)
✓ **Xu Xilin** (*Chinese revolutionary*): Taiwan Sp.256 (1988)
✓ **Xuanzang** (*Chinese Buddhist monk*): China 2016-24 & 2016-24M

Y

- ✓ **Yang Hucheng** (*Chinese general*): China 1993-16
- ✓ **Yang Shangkun** (*Chinese politician*): China 2007-18
- ✓ **Ye Jianying** (*Chinese Communist general*): China J138 (1987)
- ✓ **Ye Ting** (*Chinese Communist military leader*): China 1996-24, Macau S207 & B175 (2016)
- ✓ **Yen Chia-kan** (*Taiwan president*): Taiwan Com.250 (1994), Com.299 (2004)
- ✓ **Yu Youren** (*Chinese educator & politician*): Taiwan Sp.25 (1962)
- ✓ **Yuan Shikai** (*Chinese statesman*): Chinese Republic Com.4 (1912)
- ✓ **Yue Fei** (*Song dynasty general*): China 2003-17

Z

- ✓ **Zhan Tianyou** (*Chinese railroad engineer*): China C87 (1961), Taiwan Com.69 (1961)
- ✓ **Zhang Qian** (*Western Han dynasty diplomat*): China 2017-24 & 2017-24M
- ✓ **Zhang Wentian** (*Chinese politician*): China J170 (1990)
- ✓ **Zhang Zuolin** (*Chinese marshal*): Chinese Republic Com.7 (1928)
- ✓ **Zheng Chenggong** (Koxinga, *Ruler of Formosa*): Taiwan Def.75 (1950), Air.11 (1950), Def.79 (1953), Com.78 (1962), China 2001-27, Com.312 (2008)
- ✓ **Zheng He** (Cheng Ho, *Ming dynasty explorer*): China J113 (1985), 2005-13 & 2005-13M, Hong Kong 2005, Macau S067 & B060 (2005), Taiwan Com.248 (1994)
- ✓ **Zheng Guanying** (*Qing dynasty reformer*): Macau S033 & B030 (2002)
- ✓ **Zheng Shiliang** (*Chinese revolutionary*): Taiwan Sp.181 (1982)
- ✓ **Zhou Enlai** (*Chinese politician*): China J13 (1977), 1998-5
- ✓ **Zhu De** (*Chinese general*): Liberated Areas, China J19 (1977), J134 (1986)
- ✓ **Zhu Xi** (*Song dynasty philosopher & politician*): China 2016-26
- ✓ **Zhuge Liang** (*Ancient Chinese military strategist*): China 2014-18 & 2014-18M
- ✓ **Zou Rong** (*Chinese revolutionary*): Taiwan Sp.216 (1985)
- ✓ **Zou Taofen** (*Chinese journalist*): China J112 (1985)

Multiples

- ✓ Six Martyrs stamps of Chinese Republic (1931 – 1949)
- ✓ Famous Men of World Culture: China C25 (1953)
- ✓ Ancient Chinese Scientists: China C33 & C33M (1955), C92 (1962), J58 (1980), 2002-18, Hong Kong 2015
- ✓ Modern Chinese Scientists: China J149 (1988), J173 (1990), 1992-19, 2006-11, 2011-14, 2014-25, 2016-11
- ✓ Chinese Emperors: Taiwan Sp.27 (1962)
- ✓ Famous Chinese: Taiwan Sp.35 (1965), Taiwan Sp.41 (1966), Taiwan Sp.64 (1970), Taiwan Sp.513 (2007), Sp.641 (2016), Macau S136 & B123 (2011)
- ✓ Chinese Poets: Taiwan Sp.45 (1967)
- ✓ Chinese Cultural Heroes: Taiwan Def.96 (1972)
- ✓ Martyrs during the Sino-Japanese War: Taiwan Sp.116 (1975)
- ✓ Brilliant Chinese Women: China J27 (1978)
- ✓ Ancient Chinese Writers: China J91 (1983), 1994-9, 2013-23, 2015-6
- ✓ Friends of Chinese People: China J112 (1985)
- ✓ Noted Figures of the Xinhai Revolution: China J182 (1991)
- ✓ Democratic Patriots: China 1993-2, 1994-2
- ✓ Film Stars & Pop Singers: Hong Kong 1995, 2001, 2005
- ✓ Taiwan President & Vice-President: Taiwan Com.259 (1996), Com.276 (2000), Com.296 (2004), Com.311 (2008), Com.323 (2012)
- ✓ New Millennium: China 1999-20
- ✓ Ancient Chinese Philosophers: China 2000-20
- ✓ Early Leaders of the Chinese Communist Party: China 2001-11, 2006-14, 2011-3
- ✓ Early Generals of the People's Army: China 2002-17, 2005-26, 2012-18
- ✓ The Society of Jesus: Macau S083 & B075 (2006)
- ✓ Ethics & Moral Values: Macau S093 & B085 (2007)
- ✓ Foreign Musicians: China 2010-19, 2017-22
- ✓ Modern Chinese Musician: China 2012-4

Besides the themes listed above, there are so many other themes that collectors can come up with, based on their own interest and life experience. Stamp collecting is an art. Just let your imagination freely fly!

*

*   *

Let me briefly share with you a few more themes that are catching up in popularity:

- ✓ Buddha: Quite a number of nice issues in the market, in which the most outstanding is China's T74 (avg. $7) & T74M (avg. $40) of 1982: Color Sculpture of Liao Dynasty.

- ✓ Dunhuang Murals
    - o China's T116 (avg. $5) & T116M (avg. $20) of 1987
    - o China T26 of 1988 (less than $5)
    - o China T150 of 1990 (less than $5)
    - o China 1992-11 & 1992-11M (less than $5)
    - o China 1994-8 (less than $5)
    - o Hong Kong 2011 (less than $5)

- ✓ Buildings & monuments: Many sets have been issued. I'd highlight the following sets:
    - o China T31 (avg. $8) & T31M (avg. $300) – 1978: Highway Arch Bridges
    - o China T38 (avg. $15) & T38M (avg. $150) – 1979: The Great Wall

- ✓ Legends & Myths: Mostly from Macau. Some of the sets are catching up in value (Kun Iam 1995, Ma Chou 1998 etc.).

- ✓ I Ching Pa Kua: 8 Macau issues between 2001 and 2012. Each issue consists of an eight-value sheetlet and a miniature sheet. The average cost of acquiring the complete series is about $100.

- ✓ Archaeology: I'd highlight T88 (avg. $8) & T88M (avg. $50) – 1983 (Terracotta Army in the Tomb of Emperor Qin Shihuang).

- ✓ Flowers: Besides S44 (Chrysanthemums – 1960) and S61 (Peonies – 1963), pay attention to the following issues:
    - o China T37 (avg. $30) & T37M (avg. $200) – 1979: Yunnan Camellias
    - o China T54 (avg. $60) & T54M (avg. $300) – 1989: Lotus

The rest should be manageable within your budget.

Chapter Summary

You may recall that we concluded Chapter 3 with a table showing the development of Chinese philately. In this chapter, we take a more horizontal approach, in which each part of the chapter covers a particular period of time, and analyze concurrent philatelic issues within those timeframes in greater details. There's also a "Thematic" approach that spans almost all the timeframes.

Since this is a long chapter, let's just summarize it in the following table.

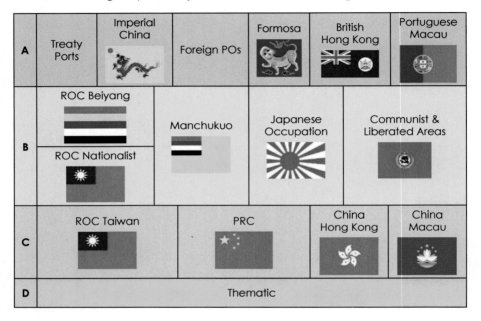

A	Treaty Ports	Imperial China	Foreign POs	Formosa	British Hong Kong	Portuguese Macau
B	ROC Beiyang / ROC Nationalist		Manchukuo	Japanese Occupation		Communist & Liberated Areas
C	ROC Taiwan		PRC		China Hong Kong	China Macau
D	Thematic					

Chapter 5
Building Your China Stamp Collection

If you intend to start building your China stamp collection, I can recommend the following 6 steps as an action plan:

Step 1: Defining your collection focus
Step 2: Getting the right catalogue
Step 3: Set a budget and timeline
Step 4: Sourcing
Step 5: Organizing your collection
Step 6: Improving your collection

Step 1: Defining Your Collection Focus

First and foremost, you need to decide what you want to collect. This is very important because it will determine which catalogue you should buy, how much you would set for your budget and how you would organize your collection.

You can collect by period. This takes a lot of time, effort and huge budget. For example:

- Qing Dynasty (might or might not include Treaty Ports)
- Foreign Post Offices in China
- Chinese Republic (might or might not include Japanese Occupation)
- Manchukuo
- People's Republic of China (might or might not include Liberated Areas)
- Republic of China (Taiwan)
- Hong Kong
- Macau

You can focus on completing one or more of the PRC series: C, S, W, Numbered, J, T and Yearly. Some appear to be much easier to complete than others. You can also consider collecting the souvenir sheets in each series.

Specializations such as Liberated Areas, Treaty Ports and Foreign post offices in China can also be a big topic that takes time and effort to build.

Cultural Revolution is another costly area to complete.

Besides, collecting by themes is another interesting way to get started. You don't need to spend as much time, effort and money if you decide to follow this direction. Some examples can be found below:

- Famous People: Sun Yat-sen/ Mao Zedong/ Chiang Kai-shek/ Lu Xun/ Karl Marx/ Lenin
- Famous People: Multiple or Individuals
- Zodiac
- Sports & Activities
- Chinese Opera
- Chinese Paintings
- Literature
- Buildings and Monuments

- Scenery
- Historical Events
- Flags
- Maps
- Flowers
- Animals
- Surcharge, etc.

You can also consider collecting only mint stamps, or only used stamps, or a mixture of both as long as it is completed. Some people have an interesting idea of collecting both mint and used. This will definitely cost an arm and a leg. Personally, I will take in anything whether it is mint or used, as long as my sets are completed.

Step 2: Getting the Right Catalogue

Once you know what to collect. It's time to get a catalogue.

There are so many China stamps catalogue out there. Some are just the duplication of others. In this section, I will introduce to you the finest China stamp catalogues in the market, and which one you should choose based on the focus that you have decided in Step 1. You can acquire all of them. But it will be a costly option.

At least will you need one or two of the following catalogues. It is very important to know what you are collecting, also to avoid overpaying and minimize your chance of bumping into forgeries and bogus.

1) Scott Catalogue

The latest 2018 edition is now available in stamp shops, on Amazon, eBay, or on Scott's online store www.amosadvantage.com.

China and Taiwan belongs to Volume 2A (countries C through Cur). In this new edition, almost 350 value changes were made among the classic issues of China. Value changes for stamps from 1878 through the early 1900s reflect a strong market, with many increases in values, some substantial. The issues of the People's Republic of China continue to show strength, but the stamps no longer are setting record prices. Overall values are slipping, except for values of great rarities. Decreases occur among the Cultural Revolution issues.

Hong Kong belongs to Volume 3 (countries G to I). The market for Hong Kong stamps is not as robust as it used to be, but the stamp values continue to reflect a strong and active market.

Macau belongs to Volume 4 (countries J to M). Value changes for classic and modern issues of Macau reflect mostly increases.

The books are thick and costly; about $125 each. If you only want the China portion of the catalogue, get the e-copy at www.scottonline.com. The price is $23. It includes both PRC and ROC, and Imperial Chinese. Hong Kong and Macau is not available in electronic edition.

Besides, there's an eBay seller by the name "<u>chirokmd</u>" who offers partial sale of the Scott catalogue. The pages are carefully removed from the main book itself. The China portion is on sale at $32, Hong Kong $7 and Macau $5.

2) Stanley Gibbons Catalogue

The latest edition was published in 2015. The catalogue is entitled "Part 17: China including Hong Kong, Macau and Taiwan". Currently, this is the only catalogue published in English which covers all the stamp issues of China in a single volume, including Liberated Areas, Japanese Occupation, Foreign Post Offices in China, Tibet, Chinese Post Office in Korea, China Expeditionary Force in Burma and India, Municipal Posts of Treaty Ports, and Machukuo.

Latest retail price is £37 (approximately $49). You can get the latest copy of this catalogue in stamp shops, on Amazon, eBay or www.stanleygibbons.com.

3) CS Philatelic (Singapore)'s Catalogue

The first and latest edition of this catalogue was published in 2015. Thanks to the great effort of Mr. Tan Chun Lim, we have another great reference resource for China stamps after 1949. This catalogue can be purchased from CS's website www.cs.com.sg at $36.

4) PPTPH's Catalogues

Published by the People's Post & Telecommunication Publishing House (PPTPH), these catalogues come in two main volumes.

- Postage Stamp Catalogue of the Republic of China (1912 – 1949). Latest edition was published in 2012. Price: ¥150 (approximately $23)

- Postage Stamp Catalogue of the People's Republic of China. Latest edition was published in 2015. Price: ¥180 (approximately $28). This book also includes China Hong Kong (1997 – 2015) and China Macau (1999 – 2015)

They can be found in stamp shops, book stores, might be available on eBay and Amazon. They can also be ordered directly from PPTPH.

5) Yang Catalogue

Published by published by Yang's Stamp Service of Hong Kong, this catalogue comes in three parts:

- Yang's Postage Stamp Catalogue of the People's Republic of China (Liberated). The latest edition was published in 1998. This book is quite hard to buy nowadays

- Yang's Postage Stamp Catalogue of the People's Republic of China, Part II. The latest edition was published in 2011. Available on eBay and Amazon. Some stamp shops might still keep the stock

- Yang's Postage Stamps and Postal History Catalogue of Hong Kong. The latest edition was published in 2016. Available in stamp shops, on eBay and Amazon

Besides, the Yang Macau catalogue is also available for collectors who are specialized in this area. It is available in stamp shops, on eBay and Amazon.

6) Chan Catalogue

Fully named "Colour-illustrated Stamp Catalogue of China 1878-1949", updated based on the original works by Dr. Chan Shiu Hon, in two volumes. The latest edition was published in 2010.

It covers all periods of philately prior to the People's Republic of China, including Qing dynasty, Republic of China and Provinces, and many specialized sections such as Anti-Bandit Overprints, Manchukuo & Local Overprints, Japanese Occupation of China. There are 2 editions for you to choose from: Ordinary (soft cover) and Deluxe (hard cover).

	Ordinary edition	Deluxe edition
Volume 1	HK$400 (US$50)	HK$500 (US$65)
Volume 2	HK$300 (US$40)	HK$400 (US$50)

You can find the catalogues in stamp shops, sometimes on eBay and Amazon, and a few other websites. You can also contact Zurich Auction House in Hong Kong to order these two books.

7) China Stamp Society Catalogue (CSS)

This first edition was published in 2016, edited by James Maxwell based on the Ma Catalogue, this edition contains specialized listing for the Imperial issues of 1878 through the Republic issues of 1949, with thousands of varieties and previously unlisted stamps being included. Retail price: $70.

Official Postal Seals (1899-1948) and the Postal Savings stamps (1919-44) have also been included in this catalogue.

8) Taiwan Catalogue

Edited by Alex Yeh, this is the most popular Taiwan stamp catalogue to be circulated in the stamp collecting world. It covers all Taiwan issues from 1945 until recently. The latest edition was published in 2017. This book cost about $20.

9) Macau Catalogue

The latest edition was published in 2015. It covers all Macau issues from 1884. This book cost about $20.

From a collector's point of view, each catalogue has their own strengths and weaknesses, depending on your collection scope and preference. For your reference and comparison, below is my analysis on each catalogue.

	Convenience	Inconvenience
Scott	* Decent layout and easy to use * Wide coverage with great details * Scott identification number are among the most popular in the philately world * There is an electronic version for China * Updated every year	* Only displays the image of one stamp in each set * No correlation of PRC's series number (C, S, J, T etc.) * Limited elaboration on reprint issues * The physical book is quite costly and bulky * No electronic editions of Hong Kong and Macau

Stanley Gibbons	* The only catalogue published in English which covers all the stamp issues of China in a single volume * Value for money * Great level of details with decent layout and interesting historical reference * Convenient size to bring along	* Only displays the image of one stamp in each set * No correlation of PRC's series number (C, S, J, T etc.) * Limited elaboration on reprint issues * Quite complex for newbies to navigate
CS Philatelic	* Images of all stamps are clearly displayed for every set * Many useful elaboration on reprint issues, some of which cannot be found in other catalogues * Convenient size to bring along * Affordable price	* Only specialized in PRC issues after 1949 * Might not be easily accessible in certain parts of the world * For the time being, it needs to be shipped from Singapore
PPTPH	* Images of all stamps are clearly displayed for every set * Some of the details might not be found in other catalogues (for example, quantity issues, designer etc.)	* Most of the details are written in Chinese (simplified) * Only shows the value of mint stamps for PRC issues * Does not cover Hong Kong before 1997, Macau before 1999 and Manchukuo * Last updated in 2012-2013. Value might not be up-to-date
Yang Catalogue	* Written in both English and Chinese * Images of all stamps are clearly displayed in every set * Finest reference for Liberated Area specialization * Convenient size to bring along	* Might not be easily accessible in certain parts of the world * PRC volume hasn't been updated for a while. Liberated volume hasn't been updated for more than 10 years, is currently out of print and very hard to find
Chan Catalogue	* One of the leading reference to be used in Asia, especially during auctions * Brief introduction of each and every issue. Many details cannot be found in other catalogues * Written in both English and Chinese (traditional) * Elaboration on postage rate in different periods	* Quite costly * Only covers the period from 1878 to 1949, mainly Imperial and Republic era * Last updated in 2010. Value might not be up-to-date
CSS Catalogue	* Detailed illustration on varieties that haven't been included in any other catalogues in the market * Historical and socio-political information has been added to accompany the philatelic aspect of the material	* Only suitable for collectors of pre-1949 China stamps * For the time being, it needs to be shipped from the US * Printing and binding are a little bit casual (ring-binded with laminated cover page)

Taiwan Catalogue	* Images of all stamps are clearly displayed in every set * Convenient size to carry along * Affordable	* Most of the details are written in Chinese (traditional) * Only specialized in Taiwan issues
Macau Catalogue	* Images of all stamps are clearly displayed in every set * Convenient size to carry along * Affordable	* Only written in Chinese * Only specialized in Macau issues

If you are on budget and want only PRC materials, CS Philately's catalogue is sufficient. Chinese speakers might want to get the PRC volume of PPTPH catalogue.

If you're looking at Manchukuo as a starting point, Chan catalogue or Stanley Gibbons could be the good option.

If you're focusing on Communist Liberated Area, try to look for the relevant volume of the Yang catalogue, though it is not quite easy to get the book these days.

If your attention is on Imperial and Republic period, get the Chan catalogue, or the ROC volume of PPTPH catalogue.

Hong Kong collectors can get the latest Yang catalogue instead of buying the entire Scott Volume 3 just for the Hong Kong portion. Same for Macau collectors, who are better off getting the Macau catalogue alone.

Taiwan collectors will just go ahead and grab a copy of Yeh's catalogue.

If you don't have a tight budget, or if your scope of collection is wide enough, you might get more than one catalogue.

Last but not least, let's summarize the catalogues in the table below based on 7 attributes, on the rating scale of 1-5. 1 is the least appealing and 5 is the most appealing to each attribute.

	Scott	Stanley Gibbons	CS	PPTPH	Yang	Chan	CSS	Taiwan	Macau
Coverage	4	5	1	2	3	2	3	1	1
Details	3	4	2	4	4	4	5	3	3
Visual	2	2	5	5	5	5	5	5	5
Recency	5	4	4	4	1	2	4	5	4
Price	2	3	5	4	4	2	4	5	5
Size	1	4	5	3	5	2	4	5	5
Availability	5	5	3	3	1	2	2	4	4

Step 3: Setting Your Budget and Timeline

Based on your collecting preference, you can set a budget according to the estimates given in the catalogues.

Don't be too ambitious if you just started unless you can afford huge budget. For example, you can set a target of completing C and S series in one year, and your budget is $2,000. That means you only need to spare an average amount of less than $200 per month for your project.

Of course, you can shorten the timeline depending on your financial power, or set aside a lump sum. Sometimes, you'll be better off upon coming across a great deal.

If you already have a lot of China stamps, start referring to the catalogue and determine what is missing, and set your timeline to get your collection completed.

Step 4: Sourcing Your China Stamp Collection

Since this is a big topic, let's talk about it in greater details in a separate chapter.

Step 5: Organizing Your Collection

Choosing the Suitable Accessories

The most popular method is to store your collection in stamp stockbooks. Lighthouse is among the best brands of philatelic accessories nowadays. You can view a wide range of their products on their website www.leuchtturm.com. However, they might not ship directly to your country. In this case, you need to find their distribution agent in your country, most of whom are stamp dealers. Or you can search for the relevant products on eBay or Amazon.

One disadvantage of storing your stamps in stockbooks is that you can't really customize the size of your album pages because each page has a fixed number of lines. Sometimes, your medium to large size stamps occupy more than one line in the page. In this case, you can look into stock pages with different pocket size. Most of the stock page is in A4 size.

I would highly recommend Lighthouse's Vario stock pages, ranging from one to eight lines each page. It is available in one-sided (C ranges – clear page) or two-sided (S ranges – black page). The good thing about Vario stock page is that it is made of plastic, which is perfect to store mint stamps or CTO stamps with gum. If you store the stamps in stockbooks, extra protection methods might be required to avoid the stamps being stuck on the album page, especially in countries with high humidity. Below are common sizes of Vario stock pages for stamps:

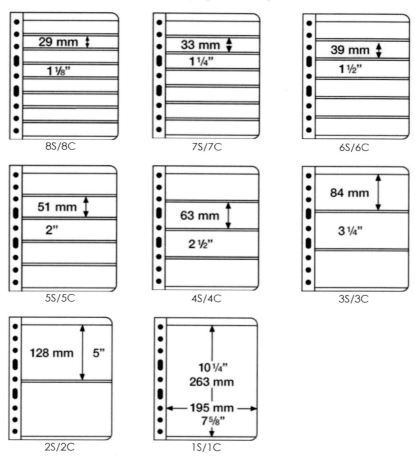

You can keep the stock pages in a decent-looking binder.

Besides, I would also recommend Hagner stock pages, existing in different sizes, either single-sided or double-sided. Just type "Hagner stock sheets" or "Hagner stock pages" in Google and you will find many online retailers that offer this product. Do avoid using Hagner for stamps with gum because it is made of paper.

You can also display your stamps on preprinted album pages. A common album page includes black-and-white or colored pictures of the stamps, with a thin frame around each stamp. In the old time, people used hinges to mount the stamps on the page. Nowadays, we can use pre-cut mounts to stick to the page. The most convenient type is "hingeless album" system where the pockets are mounted on the album page and you just need to slot your stamps in. This type is very costly. A complete Scott China stamp album cost over $700.

You can find these stamp albums on eBay, Amazon, or on www.ihobb.com.

You can download the free album pages of Chinese Empire, Chinese Republic and Taiwan from the link below. No image is displayed on the pages: http://www.chinastampsociety.org/free-stamp-album-pages

Organizing Your Stamps

If you are using preprinted album, it is very simple. You just need to slot the stamps in the spaces provided. Labelling and organizing the stamps in an appropriate order has been taken care by the album manufacturer. They even design nice cover page and include detailed descriptions on the album pages. You don't need to work so hard in this case.

If you are using stockbooks or stock pages, you need to organize the stamps to suit the concept that you have initially adopted. You might also want to label the stamps properly, add the page number, and create labels for the cover of the albums, especially when the collection fills up more than one stockbooks. This requires a lot of work but the learning path is extremely fulfilling. You will definitely gain very high sense of satisfaction and appreciation after the tremendous effort to put the collection together.

Below are a few examples of how a collection is organized in stockbooks:

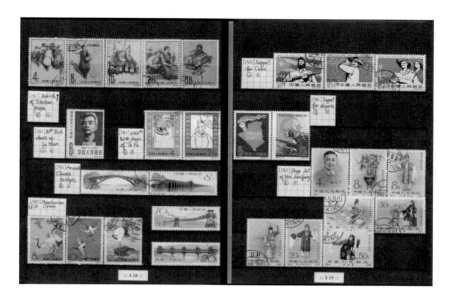

Step 6: Improving Your Collection

When you have completed organizing your collection, ask yourself whether you are satisfied with what you have; or you would like to take your collection to the next level. If you want to improve your collection, how you should go about.

A few suggestions...

You can expand the scope of your collection by widening the timeframe of your collection, or venturing into a totally new area that you've never explored before.

You can embark on a new theme and start over again. It is just a brand-new journey!

You can consider collecting miniature sheets of the issues that you are currently have.

You can start looking at high-ticket items to improve your collection, such as errors, varieties and rarities.

Interesting ideas will come along while you are building up your collection.

Chapter 6
Buying China Stamps

Nowadays, it's no longer cheap to buy China stamps. Although some sets are still affordable, it cost an arm and a leg if you are serious in building a comprehensive collection.

In this chapter, I'm going to share with you a few sources to buy China stamps.

Sourcing the Latest Issues

First and foremost, let's stay up-to-date with the market. You will probably buy the stamps at the lowest cost possible when they are just released. As you have seen in the previous chapter, there are a lot of happenings in the market lately, mostly due to speculation activities. Many of the stamp sets can increase tremendously in value after a short period of time (especially some Zodiac issues). Buying when the stamps are just released means you pay the face value. Whether you buy it for collection or speculation, this will only do you good.

China

For latest issues of Mainland China stamps, visit http://jiyou.11185.cn. Unfortunately, there is no English option on the website. So, you'll need to click on second item in the menu (中国邮票– China stamps), then click on the first item (邮票– Stamps). It will lead to a page in which all of the latest stamps issues are listed.

If you want to check the issuing plan of the year, go to www.cpi.com.cn, then scroll all the way down and look for the "新邮预报" tab (literally meaning "Stamp Forecast"). Unfortunately, there's no English for this page either.

Click on "新邮预报", and you'll see the page below. Now, click on "发行计划" (Issuing plans).

Then click on the year that you want to see. You'll see the detailed issuing plan of the year. But it will all be in Chinese. Don't worry! Mr. Google Translate can help in some ways.

Hong Kong

I'm sure you will feel better with the Hong Kong Post website (www.hongkongpoststamps.hk). You can choose to display it in English by clicking on the top right corner of the screen!

After that, very straightforward, click on "Stamps".

Then, click "Stamp Issuing Programme".

Click on the year you want to see. And everything will just be laid out in front of you. And, the best part is, all the photos of the stamps are just right there!

Macau

The website for Macau is www.ctt.gov.mo. This site is tri-lingual (Chinese, English & Portuguese). First, just click on "Philately".

Choose "Annual Issue Programme" on the "Product Information" tab. Then click the year you want to check, you'll see the detailed issuing plan.

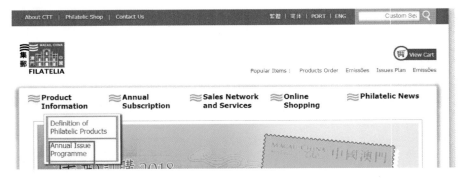

Taiwan

The page for Taiwan stamps is www.post.gov.tw. This page also has the English option on the top menu bar. Once you are on the page, click "Postal Services".

Then click "Stamp Collecting", then "Schedule for New Issue" on the left side bar. You'll see the schedule.

If you want to see all the Taiwan stamps since day one, click on "Stamp Treasure" just above that option.

Each page allows you to order the products by filling in a form or simply click on the order button. You can choose to order a few issues at a time to save on the shipping cost. Otherwise, you can also buy from a few eBay sellers and combine the shipping for all new issues from China, Hong Kong, Macau and Taiwan. I'll introduce a few of them in the next sections (with whom I have no affiliation).

That's it for new issues. How about old issues? Where and how to source? Please read on.

Buying Stamps from Collectors

Buying the entire collection from a collector is an ideal shortcut. Usually, senior collectors who have been keeping stamps for years would be more willing to let go of their collection at a lower price than catalogue value, reasons being:

- Their children and grandchildren might not appreciate stamps and don't want to seriously inherit the collection. In such cases, the collector is more than happy to pass on the collection to those who can appreciate it

- Current value of China stamps is much higher than the cost that they initially spent to build their collection. Even if they sell it at half of the catalogue value, it is still a gain to them

A few years ago, I have seen someone buying a China stamp collection from a retired collector at $10,000. If he resells that particular collection today, he might gain at least twice.

If you are part of the traditional philatelic community in your town, you might be able to get in touch with such group of collectors. Some of them do set up a booth in stamp shows to disseminate their collection.
Recently, I visited the booth of a retired collector during the International Stamp Exhibition 2015 in Singapore. Someone bought a lot from this collector that he has to use a van to transport the stamps home. I am sure this person has got a great deal.

Although acquiring stamps this way requires a significant amount of capital, the quality is almost guaranteed. You can start a collection in the fastest way possible. And it might cost much less compared to your accumulative effort of buying from different sources over the years.

Buying Stamps from Dealers

I'm sure you can find a stamp dealer in your town. In this section, I will introduce a few dealers who display China stamp as a specialization in their profile. Some of them also operate as mini auction houses. Many of them have online store or selling on eBay. I am not an affiliate of any of them; and I receive no credits to mention them in this book. Based on the reviews and credibility they received from the stamp community, I would like to introduce them to you as a resource to build your collection. Personally, I do visit some of them on a frequently basis.

Richard Tang

North America

Asia Philatelics
PO Box 730993
San Jose, CA 95173, US
Tel: +1 408 238 0893 | Fax: +1 408 238 2539
Email: richard@asiaphilatelics.com

Bick International
PO Box 854, Van Nuys, CA 91408, US
Tel: +1 818 997 6496 | Fax: +1 818 988 4337
Email: iibick@sbcglobal.net
Website: www.bickinternational.com

Bison Stamp & Coin Company
2006 N Truman Blvd
Crystal City, MO 63019-1021, US
Tel: +1 314 283 0135
Email: ppa@bisonstamps.com
Website: www.bisonstamps.com

Blackburn & Blackburn Ltd.
PO Box 321, Mt. Shasta, CA 96067, US
Email: bnbltd@aol.com

Eric Ng Philatelics
25 Ludlow St. G/F, New York, NY 10002, US
Tel: +1 212 966 6903 | Fax: +1 718 591 1026
Email: ericng8888@hotmail.com

Greg Manning
4 Whitfield Ct.
Boonton Township, NJ 07005-9537, US
Tel: +1 973 257 7214 | Fax: +1 973 257 7216
Email: gm@gregmanning.net

Jade Crown International Stamp Co. (Only PRC materials)
PO Box 118, Blaine, WA 98231-0118, US
Tel: +1 604 288 8815
Email: guanlun@hotmail.com

John H. Talman Ltd.
Box 70 Adelaide St. P.O.
Toronto ON M5C 2H8, Canada
Tel: +1 647 704 6441
Email: jtalman@interlog.com
Website: www.talmanstamps.com

Marcel Philatelic
PO Box 1596, Rancho Mirage, CA 92270, US
Tel: +1 442 227 4690 | Fax: +1 760 404 0984

Michael Rogers
4 Finance Dr. Suite 100, Danbury, CT 06810, US
Tel: +1 203 297 6056
Website: www.michaelrogersinc.com

Rising Sun Stamps
PO Box 716, Marshalls Creek, PA 18335-0716, US
Tel: +1 570 421 6043 | Fax: +1 570 421 5758
Email: haruyo_baker@msn.com

United States Stamp Company
5901 Christie Ave.
Emeryville, CA 94608, US
Tel: +1 800 509 8682
Email: ronu@pacbell.net
Website: www.usstampco.com

Washington Stamps
P. O. Box 34430, Bethesda, MD 20827, US
Tel: +1 301 493 4982 | Fax: +1 301 530 2461
E-mail: salesdept@washingtonstamps.com
Website: www.washingtonstamps.com

Singapore

China Jia Long Trading
6001 Beach Rd #02-22
Golden Mile Tower, Singapore 199589
Tel: +65 6295 2777 | Fax: +65 6295 3608
Email: chinajialong96@gmail.com

CS Philatelic Agency (Editor of the CS China catalogue)
3 Coleman Street #04-29
Peninsula Shopping Centre, Singapore 179804
Tel: +65 6337 1859, +65 6339 9584 | Fax: +65 6337 0881
Email: info@cs.com.sg
Website: www.cs.com.sg

Fang Zheng Trading
60 Eu Tong Sen Street #01-06
Furama Hotel Shopping Centre, Singapore 059804
Tel: +65 6438 2081 | Fax: +65 6438 2086
Email: fzcollections@hotmail.com
Website: www.fz-collection.com.sg

Happy Philatelic Agency
6001 Beach Rd #B1-51
Golden Mile Tower, Singapore 199589
Tel: +65 6296 0020, +65 6298 5944 | Fax: +65 6298 5512
Email: enquiries@happyphilatelic.com
Website: www.happyphilatelic.com

Lee Mui Department Store
144 Bukit Timah Road #02-16
Beauty World Centre Singapore 588177
Tel: +65 6467 0287

Europe

China Philately Ltd.
P.O. Box 48, Daventry
Northamptonshire, NN111UP, United Kingdom
Tel: +44 13 27 876438 | Fax: +44 13 27 876438
Email: chinastamps@btinternet.com

D&O Trading
PO Box 97, 9800 AB Zuidhorn
The Netherlands
E-mail: info@dandotra.com
Website: www.dandotra.com

Hans-J. Graessler
Bürgerstr. 12, 53173 Bonn - Bad Godesberg
Nordrhein-Westfalen, Germany
Tel: +49 228 353556 | Fax: +49 228 353562
Website: www.graessler-auction.com

Stampdile Ltd.
PO Box 72, Harrow
Middlesex, HA2 9XJ, United Kingdom
Tel: +44 20 8429 4222 | Fax: +44 20 8429 1477
Email: stampdile@aol.com
Website: www.stampdile.com

Hong Kong

Yang's Philatelic Trading Co.
Flat/Rm 1525, 15/F, Star House,
3 Salisbury Road, Tsim Sha Tsui, Hong Kong
Tel: +852 2317 7428
E-mail: info@yangsphil.com
Website: www.yangsphil.com

Luen Fat Stamp Shop
Shop 204 Ho Mong Kok Shopping Centre
167-173 Portland Street, Kowloon, Hong Kong
Tel: +852 9317 4899 | Fax: +852 2332 8302
Email: info@luenfat88.com
Website: www.luenfat88.com

Sun Fei Coins & Stamps Co. Ltd.
Shop 150, Ho Mong Kok Shopping Centre
169-173 Portland Street, Kowloon, Hong Kong
Email: info@sunfeico.com
Webiste: www.sunfeico.com

Treasure-Hunters Ltd.
Rm 1003, 10/F, Wellborne Commercial Centre
8 Java Road, North Point, Hong Kong
Tel: +852 2507 3773, +852 2507 5770 | Fax: +852 2519 6820
Email: exlpoon@gmail.com
Website: www.chinastampexperts.com

China

Shanghai Jianjun Stamp Shop
5th Floor, A15 & C2, Yunzhou Curio City
88 Damuqiao Rd
Xuhui, Shanghai, 200032, China
Email: hejianjun@888stamp.com
Website: www.888stamp.com

Shanghai Wencheng Stamp Shop
758 Guilin Rd
Xuhui, Shanghai, 200233, China
Tel: +86 21 6417 9972 | Fax: +86 21 6417 9972
Email: 876091270@qq.com

Topical World Stamp Co.
5th Floor, Tower 12, Hedi Lanwan 200
South Ma' anshan Rd, Hefei, 230002, China
Tel: +86 551 6288 3820 | Fax: +86 551 6561 9572
Email: info@topicalworld.com
Website: www.topicalworld.com

Taiwan

Shuang He Philatelic
90 Chongqing South Road, Section 2
Taipei, Taiwan
Tel: +886 2 2332 8828 | Fax: +886 2 2332 6649
Email: chang1800@yahoo.com.tw

Qing Shui Philatelic
239-1 Chungshan Road, Qingshui District
Taichung 436, Taiwan
Tel: +886 4 2622 6997 | Fax: +886 4 2622 3606
Email: po38ts43699@yahoo.com.tw

Buying Stamps Online

Thanks to modern technology, buying stamps online has never been easier and more convenient. There are so many quality platforms where you can source for stamps. In this section, I will introduce the platforms that I find the most efficient and reliable.

You just need to keep coming back to these sites and you will be able to find good stamps every now and then.

eBay

eBay is by far the most popular online shopping site globally until 2015 when Alibaba took over their top position. Billions of transactions take place on eBay every year. To date, eBay is no stranger to stamp collectors globally. You can find many great deals on eBay.

I will share with you some tips to buy China stamps on eBay.

Usually, people will search "China stamps", "China stamps collection", "China stamp lot". I will show you advanced keywords for more refined search results. For the time being, let's take "China stamp collection" as an example:

The result will show the whole list of currently listed China stamp lots. Most of the time, these will be loose lots and you will need to add in tremendous efforts if you want to take it up from there.

Below are some results I received for this search. For such a loose lot, the highest bidding is already at $86. When the auction ends, the hammer price is expected to reach no less than $100. There are also items that you can buy right away instead of bidding.

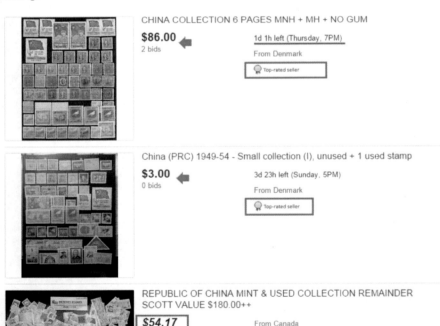

CHINA COLLECTION 6 PAGES MNH + MH + NO GUM

$86.00
2 bids

1d 1h left (Thursday, 7PM)
From Denmark
Top-rated seller

China (PRC) 1949-54 - Small collection (I), unused + 1 used stamp

$3.00
0 bids

3d 23h left (Sunday, 5PM)
From Denmark
Top-rated seller

REPUBLIC OF CHINA MINT & USED COLLECTION REMAINDER SCOTT VALUE $180.00++

$54.17
or Best Offer

From Canada
Top-rated seller

What I want to highlight here is the top-rated status of the sellers, which means they already have certain reputation in the marketplace. Let's do a quick check.

There you go! Over 10,000 feedbacks; 100% positive feedback; and more importantly, he has a store! This shows that he is a professional seller. You can go through the feedback on his profile to gain more insights. You can see from the records how many China lots he has been selling lately and what people said about his products. Also, do take a look at his listings to find out how many China lots that he is currently selling. From there, you can evaluate the quality of his items.

Some sellers might have received a few negative feedbacks. In this case, just click and see what happened. Sometimes, a few negative feedbacks don't really mean the seller is not reliable. We encounter unhappy people (both reasonable and unreasonable) on every corner of life!

Besides looking at the seller profile, we should also look into the following factors to determine whether the item is worth a buy:

✓ Item description: Whether it is detailed or brief. Any highlight on defects. How knowledgeable the seller is can be observed by his choice of words, the terminologies and jargons he uses in the listing

✓ Photos: How many photos being displayed. Whether the photos are clear enough for you to see the condition of the stamps

✓ Return policy: If the seller offers return policy, this means he is confident that you'll be happy with the item. If return is not accepted, you should try to find out what's wrong with the lot before placing a bid

✓ Contact the seller if you have any question. Observe how the seller answers your questions. How responsive he is

The disadvantage of buying from a high-rated seller is that the auction can be quite competitive. These sellers usually have a big group of followers, who are ready to click on the bid button any time when there's new listing. Price usually goes wild upon the end of the auction. Many people will only place their bid towards the very last seconds of the auction.

If you want to get a good deal, you can consider buying from new sellers as well although they haven't got a very good profile in the market. You just need to consider the 4 factors mentioned above to enter the trade. The most important thing is the return policy offered by these new sellers.

Search filter is another useful function that I would like to highlight. If you want to see only "auction" or "buy it now" transaction, click on the relevant buttons on the top left corner just above the product list.

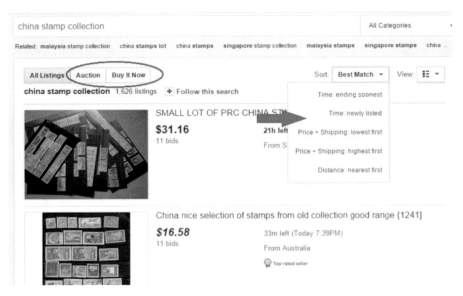

For "buy it now" transaction, you can sort by price in ascending order. For auctions, you can sort by ending soonest so that you don't have to wait for days.

Advanced collectors will have a different set of keywords when they conduct a search on eBay. You can use Scott numbers, series number and other keyword related to the topic of the stamps to conduct the search.

Below are a few examples. When I keyed in "China S38" (The famous Gold Fish issue), I got the following results:

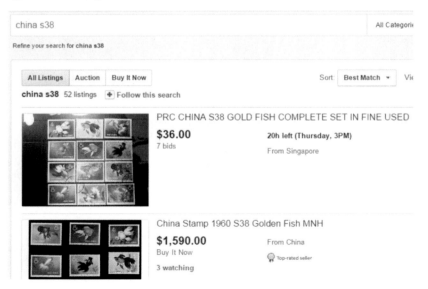

7 ongoing bids for the used set; and the bidding will go even crazier towards the end of the listing. 3 people were watching the mint set. Not bad, right?

Let's take a look at another example. When I keyed in "China C122", the result came out as the screenshot below. I'll probably grab the MNH set right away if I am yet to have it. Please refer to chapter 4 for the fair value of this set.

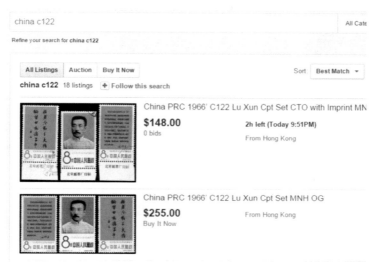

Below is another example with the keyword "1966 China Sc#919" (if I know the Scott number of the stamp).

As you go along and become more experienced, you will have more keyword ideas for your search.

I would recommend some of the following sellers who have quite a comprehensive stocks of China stamps, especially new issues. They have always been my go-to over the last few years. The more important part is that they are reliable.

- **sungsung168**: Strong in Hong Kong and Macau, and new issues of China, especially Zodiac stamps
- **playstamp88**: Strong in Hong Kong and Macau, and new issues of China
- **ffgumming**: A lot of China issues, new and older
- **dwu2005**: Strong in Taiwan stamps, with large stocks of older issues

HipStamp

HipStamp, a Stanley Gibbons company, is an online stamp trading platform. HipStamp is yet to be as competitive as eBay and you can find a lot of great deals on the platform. It is free to use.

HipStamp is a good venue to find loose China stamps if you are looking for certain pieces to fill the gaps in your album. Let's do a quick search for the keyword "China stamps".

Below is the result I got:

There are a lot of keyword options that you can play around with, just like what I did in the previous section on eBay.

And, remember! This site is much less competitive than eBay for the time being. So, if you are involved in a bidding game, chances are that you might got some good deals.

StampWorld

StampWorld is another awesome place that I would like to introduce to you. This site allows collectors all over the world to buy and sell stamps. You can also find many reliable dealers on this site. Just register for an account and it is free.

Like HipStamp, you may be able to find good quality China stamps, in complete set or loose, at a good price.

To search for stamps, click on the "Buy Stamps" button, then choose "Buy single stamps or sets".

Click on "Asia", then "China", and you will have thousands of items to choose from.

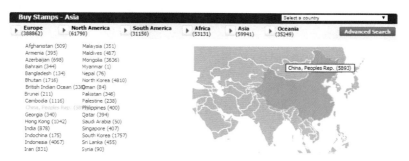

You can also find thousands of items under Hong Kong, Macau and Taiwan separately.

When buying on StampWorld, try to look for multiple items from the same seller to save on the shipping cost.

Delcampe

Delcampe is another online platform for collectibles buyers and sellers. Like eBay and HipStamp, they offer both "buy now" and "bid" options. You'll be able to find a lot of China stamps on this page as well.

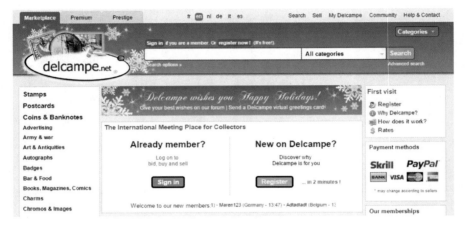

100Surplus

While introducing 100Surplus, I would highlight that it might not be as resourceful as the sites introduced earlier. But once in a while, you can find C and S series stamps at good price. J and T issues can easily been found on this page as well.

You can try the keyword techniques that I shared earlier to conduct a search on 100Surplus. Remember to keep coming back and search for good deals here!

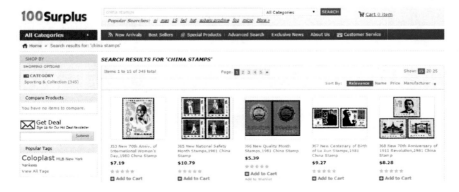

AliExpress

AliExpress is another site that has quite a number of China stamps for sale.

You can compare the price with the value guide in this book or in your catalogue while making a deal on this page.

[01060]China Stamps W6 Chairman Mao the Red Sun.	**[04107]PR china 1968 stamp w12 chairman mao goes to An	**[04118] R P china 1967 stamp w2 Long Live Chairman Mao.
US $25.80 / piece	US $42.69 / Set	US $32.29 / piece
Shipping US $2.11 / piece	Shipping US $2.11 / Set	Shipping US $2.11 / piece

ZhaoOnline

ZhaoOnline is an online auction website, fully specialized in China collectible materials. Here you can find various items from low to high-end. A lot of good quality items can be found on this site. Yet it is quite competitive.

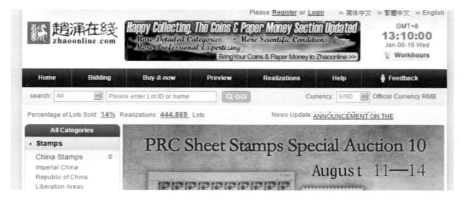

XABusiness

If you are collecting new China stamps, XABusiness is a great resource. However, most of the old items are displayed as "out of stock" on this site.

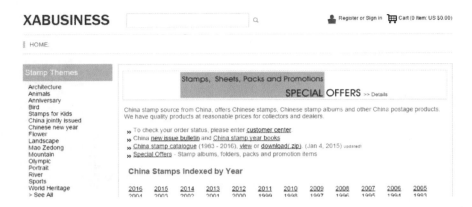

Buying Stamps in Exhibitions

There are many advantages of buying stamps in local shows or regional/ international exhibitions. First of all, you have a wide variety of choice to choose from. You can also bargain for a good deal when purchasing in bulk. Sellers can be stamp dealers or retired collectors that I have mentioned in the previous part.

However, you tend to overspend in such events because you have way more choices than you can imagine.

Buying Stamps in Auctions

Most of the stamps sold in auctions have the investment quality. If you are an advanced collector who are looking for rare stamps to fill the vacant spots in your album, then auction is a venue for you. I will discuss a little more in details when we come to the chapter on investment.

Sometimes, auction houses also carry lots of estate collection. Some of the lots can be quite solid. You can also consider this option to fast-track your collection journey. High capital is required for sure.

Stamp Exchange

Stamp exchange is usually carried out in a traditional philatelic community. This method is quite helpful when you have extra stamps and look for certain pieces to fill up the gaps in your album. However, I have seen less and less of these activities happening in this date and age.

*
* *

We'll conclude this chapter by comparing the pros and cons of buying China stamps from the sources that have been mentioned.

	Pros	Cons
Buying from collectors	* The hard work has been done for you so that you don't need to start from scratch * You might get a good deal, paying less for a high quality collection * You can learn from the experience of the seller	* You might need significant amount of capital to start
Buying from dealers	* You can control the quality of what you will get, because you can see it with your own eyes * You may learn from the experience of the seller	* Sometimes you tend to pay much higher than buying elsewhere
Buying online	* You have access to a wide variety of choices * You may pay much lower than purchasing offline due to fierce competition among sellers	* You can't control the quality of what you buy * There's chance of getting scammed and running into forgeries
Buying in exhibitions	* You will come across many quality items * You may enjoy great discount * You may expand your connection and have a great chance to learn from experienced people	* You are overloaded with too many options * There's high chance of spending too much
Buying in auctions	* High quality items that are carefully audited by experts	* High cost due to fierce competition
Stamp exchange	* Trust and reliable * An efficient way to fill album gaps	* Not very common nowadays

Richard Tang

Chapter 7
Selling China Stamps

This chapter is for those who already have a stamp collection and want to pass it on to other collectors. If you just start, I recommend you not going into buy and sell because arbitrage doesn't really work in the collectibles market.

You can sell your collection in two ways:

- Selling the entire collection in one go
- Breaking the collection down and selling it part by part

I cannot comment which model is better. Each has its own strengths and challenges. Selling the entire collection might take a long time because it's not easy to find people who are willing to spare such huge capital to acquire it in one go. Besides, if you sell to dealers, they tend to pay you much lower than you expect. If you sell your collection in parts, you might cash it in faster. But you will experience the pain of creating gaps in your album. There are slow-moving sets in the collection that you need to let go at lower price in the end.

If you are serious to let go of your collection, I would recommend some tips that might help you to sell it more efficiently. These are the tips that I used to sell not only my China stamps, but also other stamps, FDCs and coins.

Pre-Sale

Before you sell your collection, it is important to raise awareness and create trust with your potential buyers.

Expanding Your Network

If you have been collecting stamps for a while, you might already be hanging out with a group of collectors.

Thanks to social media, you can expand your network with a click of the mouse. Simply search on Facebook with the keywords "China stamps", you will find many pages or closed group with full of China stamp collectors and enthusiasts. Another good thing when joining these communities is that you can learn a lot from fellow collectors all over the world.

Besides, you can create your own Facebook fan page to share your collection with the world.

You can take part in online discussion forums. There are not many out there. Below are two popular forums dedicated to Chinese philately:

www.chinastampsociety.org/forum
www.china-stamps.com

You can also make friends during stamp shows or with those who usually visit stamp shops in your town.

Building Your Reputation

The best way to create good reputation is to share your knowledge and experience with your peers, whether it is online or offline. Just a few minutes per day, your accumulative effort will eventually pay off. People will pay respect to you every time they see you.

If you have your Facebook stamp page, you can post nice photos or scans of your collection, share your knowledge and market observation. Most people will appreciate that a lot.

Creating Awareness among Your Audience

If you are already hanging out with a group of collectors, you might want to let them know your intention to sell your collection.

You can start posting your collection on your own Facebook page, and share the post on other fan pages or closed groups on which your have membership.

You can also "show off" your collection on the platforms listed below to expand your fan base and let people know what you have. Who knows somewhere in the world, there'll be someone who is keen on your collection and he will contact you directly:

www.popgrotto.com
www.collectorfocus.com
www.collectionmasteronline.com
www.stamporama.com/exhibits

That's the pre-sale process that has worked quite well for me. In the subsequent section, I will share with you some of the selling platforms that I used to sell my collections.

The Selling Process

Selling Stamps through Your Own Network

This is very powerful. When you're selling through your network, the level of trust has been more or less established. You simply need to pass on the message to those you know, and if possible, ask for their favor to pass on the message to those they know. China stamps are so popular nowadays that people will just contact you immediately if they know you have some to sell. I've been selling many of my extra sets. The response is very good when it comes to networking.

Selling Stamps to Dealers

If you want to quickly liquidate your collection, you can sell it to any dealers in your town. However, all dealers need to make a profit. So, even the most honest dealer will probably pay you much lower than you expect.
Most of the time, they are willing to pay only 10-20% of the catalogue value.

Dealers usually use the following reasons to negotiate:

- The condition of your stamps: Even if it is not quite bad, they will try to find some faults with the stamps to maximize the chance of paying you less

- The demand of such kinds of stamps in the market: They might claim that as day-in-day-out sellers, they have the most up-to-date market information that you don't have. They might say that your stamp is of average market demand and can only fetch average price

- The amount of stocks that they hold: They might tell you that they have a handful of what you have, and it makes little difference for them to take in your collection

- Their specialization: Some will claim that they are specialized in a different area of philately and will only take in your collection at certain price

Nowadays, stamp dealers are also selling online, in exhibitions and flea markets, etc. If they buy from you, they will sell at a higher price on other platform. While you can do it yourself, do read on. Unless you need fast cash, you might want to consider selling to dealers as the last resource.

Selling Stamps Online

In the previous chapter we have examined a few platforms from which we can buy China stamps.

Some of these platforms can also be leveraged on when it comes to selling. Most of the time, I will use these following three:

- eBay
- HipStamp
- Delcampe

You need to pay close attention to the fees and policy when selling on these sites.

eBay charges you 10% of the sale, including the shipping cost and sales tax (if you and your buyer live in certain locations). You also incur the PayPal fee of 3% applied on the final sale value plus shipping charge. In the case of cross-currency transaction, the buyer will have to incur additional cost due to PayPal marking up 3-4% on currency conversion.

eBay allows you to post certain number of listings every month that is free of charge. If you exceed that quota, a listing fee is applied. For new sellers, the payment received from buyers will be withheld for 21 days. After a certain number of transactions, PayPal stops withholding your fund.

When you get started on eBay, you are limited to only 10 listing or $500 per month, whichever comes first. You can call in to request for more. When listing on eBay, you can post 12 photos.

HipStamp is more cost efficient compared to eBay. Yet the traffic is not as good as eBay. It allows you to list 50 items per month for free. If you exceed 50, you will be charged 2c per listing. You can post up to 100 phots per listing. The final fee structure is also lower than eBay:

From 1c to $49.99: You pay 1c + 8% of the sales to HipStamp
From $50 to $999.99: You pay 5.5% of the sales to HipStamp
From $1,000 onwards: You pay 1.5% of the sales to HipStamp

Do take note of PayPal or Skrill fees separately.

Delcampe, on the other hand, doesn't charge insertion fee. You can list as many as you want to. They only charge you commission based on monthly sales.

Under $750: 5.5% x (sales) + 18c per item
From $750 to $1,499.99: 5% x (sales – 750) + 41.25 + 18c per item
From $1,500 to $7,499.99: 4.5% x (sales – 1,500) + 78.75 + 18c per item
From $7,500 to $14,999.99: 3% x (sales – 7,500) + 348.75 + 18c per item
From $15,000 onwards: 2% x (sales – 15,000) + 573.75 + 18c per item

VAT is applied accordingly on Delcampe fee; and it varies depending on your country of residence. You can check the rate with a calculator on their page. Do take note of PayPal or Skrill fees.

Besides these three platforms, you can also consider listing your stamps on other websites, such as:

Shopify allows you to set up your own online shop. If you want to become a stamp dealer, then you can consider using this platform. Otherwise, you can forget about it because you need to pay a monthly subscription to use it. But I must say it is a very convenient platform to sell online.

Catawiki is a Dutch online auction company that offers a wide range of collectibles from stamps, coins, arts, jewelry to watches and classic car. The website welcomes 12 million visitors per month on average.

You can only list your item if its expected revenue is at least €75. All auction lots start at €1 and you can put a reserved price. Catawiki charges a 15.1% commission fee of the winning bid (including VAT/sales tax). The only challenge when using this platform is that the auctioneers are very picky. You need to do a lot of work to get your item listed.

The reason why you don't see this page being introduced in the previous chapter is because there are only a limited number of China stamps offers at this point of time. If you start selling now, you face less competition.

Etsy is a platform to buy and sell handmade or vintage items. I am yet to see any interesting stamps listed on this website. But you can give it a try. It charges 20c as listing fee, and the commission of 3.5% per transaction. Do take note of PayPal fees separately.

You can also tap on classified sites to advertise your collection. I personally use **Craigslist** and **Gumtree**. You can search for a list of quality classified sites in your country. Be careful of scammers when using these sites!

Selling Stamps in Exhibitions

In an earlier chapter, we discussed about retired collectors who set up booths to sell their collection in stamp shows. This is an efficient way to sell your stamps because of the quality traffic with high propensity to spend. If you have a lot of items to sell, you can consider this method. Make sure your potential revenue at least covers the rental and setup cost.

Selling Stamps in Flea Markets

Flee market is another venue that you can sell your stamps. In our case, there are two types of flea markets: Antique flea market and general flea market. The traffic at antique flea markets is more profitable than those visiting general flea market. Depending on how reasonable the rental and operating cost are, you can consider this option if you want to give up your collection. I didn't introduce this method in the previous chapter because I have never got a good deal when buying stamps at a flea market. As a seller, you can set comparatively high price. Though people tend to bargain with you, you may usually end up earning good money at the end of the day.

Selling Stamps in Auctions

You can consign your stamps to an auction house if you have rare items in your collection. Most auction houses have unique access to high net worth collectors all over the world, who can afford to enter five-digit transactions without a second thought.

When you consign your item, auction houses have their expert to investigate it carefully before it is listed for public bidding. As a consequence, it usually takes months to work with an auction house. Besides, your item needs to suit their themes in order to be included in their auction catalogue. Most auction house only has a few auctions per year. Once you miss an auction, or your item doesn't sell, you need to wait for a few months until the next auction. If your item sells, it usually takes them up to 90 days to send you the fund. The cost of selling in auction is comparatively high. While the industry standard is 15%, most of them charge 20-25% on the hammer price. In return, you have a peace of mind when working with them because they handle all transactions in a professional manner.

If you need any expert advice, contact them via email or phone and most of the time, they will respond promptly.

Selling Stamps through Mobile App

In this date and age, mobile marketplace exists in many parts of the world. I am not quite sure what is popular in your country. But I can share with you about a mobile app in Singapore called "Carousell", which allows buyers and sellers to trade any kinds of goods. Thousands of transactions have taken place within the "Vintage and Antiques" category. I have utilized this platform over the last 4 years.

If you have such a mobile app in your country, leverage on it to sell your stamps. Again, be careful of scammers too!

To conclude the chapter, let's look at the pros and cons of selling your stamps through the channels that we have talked about.

	Pros	Cons
Selling through network	* Mutual trust * You know who you are dealing with, and where your item goes to * You can take your time and negotiate for the best win-win outcome	* You might risk losing the relationship if there's any issue arising from the deal * The transaction might take longer than expected to close
Selling to dealers	* The fastest way to give up your collection * You get paid cash on the spot * They may point out the valuable pieces in your collection that you overlook	* They might take in your item at a much lower price than expected * They may also keep quiet if they spot valuable items in your collection, and pay the average price for everything
Selling online	* Sell your item fast and get paid right away, with various payment options * Access to global buyer base who can make quick decision * Comparatively low cost	* Due to high competitive, items are probably sold at a discount * Troubles arising when mail is lost during shipping * Beware of scammers
Selling in exhibitions	* Exposure to a huge target audience base, who are almost ready to spend * Sell the item fast and collect instant cash * High chance of selling in bulk * Potential contact for future transactions	* High cost: rental, setup, operation and administration * A lot of time and effort involved * Buyers tend to bargain
Selling in flea markets	* Sell your item fast and collect instant cash * High chance of selling in bulk * Potential contact for future transactions	* Cost of rental, setup, operation and administration * Shoppers might not be target audience * Buyers tend to bargain
Selling in auctions	* Increase the exposure of your item to the auction house's database of high value buyers * Leverage on the auction house' expertise to better promote and position your item * Due to competition and buyer's appetite, your item may sell at a higher price than expected	* Most auction houses are strict in the selection of items into their catalogue * High seller's fee * Might take long time to receive your revenue * There might be extra costs such as transportation fees, photograph fees, reserve fees, and buyback fees
Selling through mobile apps	* Huge and potential market: 1.8 billion smart phone users globally in 2015 * Convenience: Quick and easy to create your listing * Comparatively low cost	* Chance of dealing with a lot of lowballers and weirdos * Beware of scammers

Chapter 8
Investing in China Stamps

You have probably heard the stories of people who laughed their way to the bank by investing in rare stamps. Have you ever wondered whether you can follow their footsteps? Definitely yes! But you need to be at least an advanced collector or expert in stamps in order to venture into rare stamp investment.

Investment-Grade Stamps

An investor usually looks at the following factors to determine the value of a stamp, and to differentiate between investment-grade stamps and normal stamps:

- ✓ Rarity and uniqueness: Only a small number of surviving examples is known to exist

- ✓ Demand: There are a healthy number of collectors in the market seeking after the item

- ✓ Quality: The stamp needs to be as perfect as possible, from the perforation, margins, the freshness of the color to the gum on the back of the stamps, no stains and no other defects

- ✓ A proof of authenticity is required

- ✓ As low cost of acquisition as possible compared to the fair value of the item

- ✓ Historical significance of the stamp, for example, the withdrawal of the "Whole Country is Red" stamp due to Taiwan being left white

- ✓ A special postmark being used on the stamp

The Chinese antiques and collectibles market is the most prominent nowadays for investors. The value of rare items has continuously broken the world record over the last 10 years. The 1878–85 Large Dragons stamps, for instance, realized at over $2 million in an auction in 2011. The 1897 Red Revenue small one-dollar stamp earned closed to $900,000 in an auction in 2013.

According to the Financial Times, Chinese investors now make up a third of the $3 billion global stamp collecting market. Chinese investors hold an average of 18% of their net worth in assets such as rare stamps, coins, fine wine, classical cars and paintings.

In a previous chapter, we look into the Stanley Gibbons China stamp index, which track the performance of 200 pieces of rare investment-grade China stamps since 1989. Growth has been substantial, with cumulative growth of 1,170% over the last 25 years, and compound annual growth of 10.7%.

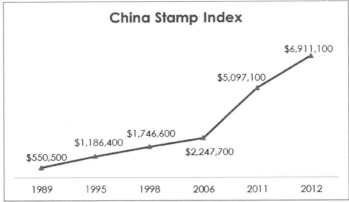

(Source: Stanley Gibbons)

The number is expected to grow further in the near future, while some of the following factors are taken into consideration:

- Historical performance: Stamps have been a powerful investment vehicle with significant growth and return. To our surprise, stamps have been performing well even during the recession

- Increasing demand:

    o Fine rare stamps are always in demand and have always fetched high price in auctions

    o The number of Chinese collectors will rise rapidly as both its population and prosperity continues to grow, especially after the end of the one-child policy and the CNY being added into IMF's elite reserve currency list

    o Non-Chinese collectors are turning their attention to China stamps. Most of them are baby-boomers, who own 80% of the world's wealth

    o As predicted by Goldman Sachs, by 2030, there will be approximately 2 billion additional people entering the middle class. This group adds a lot to the potential investor base

- Finite supply: There are only a small number of investment-grade stamps known to exist. These cannot be reproduced or replaced once lost. For example, no one can go back and print a new and authentic "Whole Country is Red" stamp

- Investor confidence: Thanks to modern technology, knowledge and information is easily accessed, increasing the level of confidence for investors

However, different people might have different opinions on stamp investment. Depending on your risk appetite and knowledge on the subject matter, you make a choice whether to stop at the collector level or venture into investing.

This chapter doesn't serve as a financial advice. It only shares the background of investing in rare stamps. The decision and action is all yours.

Building a Stamp Investment Portfolio

Since rare stamps have performed strongly and consistently over the past decades, even in times of political and economic turbulence, thousands of investors are adding them into their portfolio. People have been successful in stamps investment. Bill Gross, for example, who runs the $280 billion Pimco fund, bought $2.5 million of rare British Stamps in 2000. After 7 years, the portfolio was sold for $9.1 million.

If you have a substantial amount of capital, let's say at least $20,000, and you can wait for at least 5 years to see significant results, investing in stamps might be suitable for you.

You can work with prestigious companies such as Stanley Gibbons to start your portfolio. Stanley Gibbons has been in the collectibles market for over 150 years and is the world's leading stamp expert. Likewise, I am not credited to mention them in this book.

You can contact investment@stanleygibbons.com for more information on the different investment plans and how Stanley Gibbons can support you to growth your wealth with their expertise. They will usually respond promptly to guide you through the process.

By investing in rare stamps, you are not holding on to the stamps yourself. They will be stored in secure vaults in Stanley Gibbons' warehouse in Guernsey or Hong Kong. The stamps will be audited every year. If you want to view your stamps, request for it and they will arrange the time for you to view them.

Currently, Stanley Gibbons is offering three primary investment models:

Flexible Trading Portfolio (FTP)

You need to decide what you want to include in your trading portfolio before you start this plan. It can be a mixture of China stamps and other British Commonwealth rare stamps, or it can be only rare China stamps.

When your portfolio has been set up, you have the freedom to sell any items in your portfolio or buy more to top up any time you like.

Your share of profit will be between 30% and 80% upon exit, on top of the original investment, depending on how long you hold the portfolio:

- ✓ Up to one year: 30%
- ✓ From 1 to 3 years: 50%
- ✓ From 3 to 5 years: 70%
- ✓ Over 5 years: 80%

The remaining portion of the profit serves as commission to Stanley Gibbons.

Minimum amount of £15,000 is required for this package.

One of the investors who set up a China stamps portfolio in 2011 shared that the portfolio grew by 27% per year on average.

Capital Growth Plan (CGP)

This plan allows you to buy and hold for a contract term of 5 to 10 years, during which portfolio grows and you will receive 80% of the profit upon maturity.

When you enroll in this plan, you will be allocated a dedicated Investment Portfolio Manager who assists you to build the best portfolio structure. This person will also be your point of contact during the contract term.

This plan will lock your money for a medium to long term. However, you have the option to liquidate your investment after one year and receive 50% of the profit upon exit.

Likewise, a minimum investment of £15,000 is required for this model. Currently, Stanley Gibbons is managing a few seven-figure portfolios.

Premium Portfolio Builder (PPB)

With this plan, you will need to start with an initial investment of £10,000, adding £1,500 per quarter to grow your portfolio. There's no tie-in period. If you decide to liquidate the portfolio at any time, Stanley Gibbons will try to sell it through their database and auctions. You receive 70% of the profit.

Stanley Gibbons' experts will guide you along the way while you are building your portfolio.

Although Stanley Gibbons claim that you don't need to know about stamps to become an investor, it is recommended that you have certain knowledge to make your own judgment. The bottom line is not to invest in anything that you know nothing about.

You might come across articles written by professional financial journalists, criticizing the investment in rare stamps. While their arguments do make sense in some cases, let's not forget that we are looking into China stamps. The landscape can be way different from the general rare stamp market that they are talking about.

Thus, it is important that you study the subject matter carefully, make your own decision, and be responsible for the outcome of your decision.

Buying Stamps in Auctions

Another venue to find quality investment-grade stamps is through auctions. Stamps sold in auctions are always carefully evaluated and audited by experts before being put up for sales. So, you have the peace of mind when it comes to quality and authenticity.

Auction houses charge a buyer's premium on your winning bid. While the industry standard is 15%, you usually end up paying 20-25%. For example, if you win an item at $10,000, you need to pay an extra $2,000 (20%). So, you spend $12,000 eventually. If you bid $10,000 and opt to include the premium, they will take your bid as $8,000.

Nowadays, if you buy China stamps in auctions, you might face fierce competition from other bidders in the session.

You can visit www.stampauctionnetwork.com to find the list of upcoming auctions held by different auction houses. There are occasional auctions dedicated to China and Hong Kong materials every now and then.

Mr. Richard Lehmann, President of Income Securities Advisor, has shared some useful tips when buying at auctions. I would like to quote his words in the bullet points below:

- *Know in advance the highest price you are willing to pay for a stamp and stick to it. Remember that you are often bidding against a collector who is trying to fill a hole in his collection and will overpay to do so*

- *Try to spot the dealer bidders in the audience. Their bidding will tell you what a lot is worth and what the wholesale value is. But don't confuse a dealer with an auction agent. Such agents generally represent collectors, so they too will pay closer to a retail price. If you don't know if a bidder is a dealer, ask him*

- *Have a throw away bid in mind for any lot that is of even marginal interest. Every auction has a few steals where no-one in the room was aware and the auctioneer had a stronger interest to move on. This can happen when multiple lots of the same item come up for bid*

- *Find out the viewing schedule for lots and examine the items beforehand. Higher priced items should have a certificate as to being genuine in all respects. This means not just that it isn't bogus, but that the gum and perforations and defects are all as described (or not). Note that after you buy an item, you can request it be certified before you take delivery, for a small fee of course*

Mr. Lehmann also shared some tips on email bidding or use of an auction agent:

- *Submit only firm limit bids. In theory, you will get the lot at one increment over the highest floor or other email bid so you are encouraged to set a high limit. Don't hesitate to submit lots of throw away bids. You may get lucky on one or two. Auction houses love under bidders since it ups any higher firm bids. Auction houses offer you the ability to up your firm bid by a stated percentage, if needed. It's not needed, this option only for the must have bidder who you don't want to compete with*

- *Lots often have starting bids which may be a seller's minimum or highest firm bid. Note, however, that many auction lots may be owned by the auction house. Hence, even if you are the only bidder, your limit bid will magically be reached. This is one reason you may want to use an auction agent*

Below is a list of auction houses that hold many sessions on China materials annually:

Richard Tang

InterAsia Auction Ltd.
Suite A, 13/F, Shun Ho Tower
24-30 Ice House Street, Central, Hong Kong
Tel: +852 2868 6064 | Fax: +852 2868 6146
Email: info@interasia-auctions.com
Website: www.interasia-auctions.com

John Bull
7/F, Kwong Fat Hong Building
1 Rumsey Street, Sheung Wan, Hong Kong
Tel: +852 2890 5767 | Fax: +852 2576 5110
Email: info@jbull.com
Website: www.jbull.com

Kelleher & Rogers Ltd.
9/F, Malaysia Building , 50 Gloucester Road, Wan Chai, Hong Kong
Email: stamps@kelleherasia.com
Website: www.kelleherasia.com

Pan-Lung Philatelic
36 Nan Hai Road, Zhongzheng District, Taipei 10075, Taiwan
Tel: +886 2 2322 4499 | Fax: +886 2 2322 2166
Email: service@panlung.com.tw
Website: www.panlung.com.tw (in Traditional Chinese)

Shanghai Universe Auction Co., Ltd.
11th Floor, No.333 Zhao Jiabang Road, Shanghai, China
Tel: +86 21 5467 0188 | Fax: +86 21 5467 0177

Spink & Son
4/F and 5/F, Hua Fu Commercial Building
111 Queen's Road West, Sheung Wan, Hong Kong
Tel: +852 3952 3000 | Fax: +852 3952 3038
Email: china@spink.com
Website: www.spink.com

Zurich Asia
Room 2101-2, 21/F, 108 Java Road, North Point, Hong Kong
Tel: +852 2521 2883, +852 2563 8280 | Fax: +852 2563 8228
Email: info@zurichasia.com
Website: www.zurichasia.com

Yang's Philatelic Trading Co.
Flat/Rm 1525, 15/F, Star House,
3 Salisbury Road, Tsim Sha Tsui, Hong Kong
Tel: +852 2317 7428
E-mail: info@yangsphil.com
Website: www.yangsphil.com

Chapter 9
Final Words

Thank you again for picking up this book. And thank you for following me until the end. I hope the information in the book has added some value to you, whether you are a newbie, an intermediate to advanced collector, an investor, or simply someone who wants to know more about this subject.

If you are a yet to have a China stamp collection, it's time to start with something small. I'm sure it will be fascinating enough for you to prolong the collecting journey and learn new stuffs from this great hobby. As the collector base is still growing steadily, this area would definitely have more to offer in the coming time.

Before we end, let me share with you some of the "Dos and Don'ts" derived from my personal experience after more than 15 years of stamp collecting journey. Some of the points are for stamp collecting in general, while some are quite important if you are into China stamp collecting.

Dos

✓　Get a good catalogue. It serves as a roadmap so you won't get lost and give up. It provides a direction if you would like to expand your collection. It also helps you to define the value of your collection, avoid overpaying when you make a purchase and avoid underselling if you decide to downsize your collection

✓　Appreciate the stamps as if you own a piece of history itself. Every stamp tells a story and carries with it a unique historical value

✓　Be creative with your collection. Brainstorm the structure of your collection to make it stand out. Whether a collection can go beyond its intrinsic value depends on how it is uniquely customized

✓　Always aim to become an expert in your specialization. Not only will this enable you to assemble a solid collection, but also keep you aware of opportunities to acquire valuable items that you can eventually monetize in auctions. Being a knowledgeable person in certain areas also means you can create contents that millions of collectors and scholars will look out for. Imagine how you can create another stream of income while doing what you enjoy

✓　Join social media groups and online forums to get in touch with people who share the same interest. You will definitely learn a lot from them, and be exposed to the most up-to-date information in the market

✓　Make use of modern technology and always watch out for good deals. They are just everywhere. Imagine 30 years ago, if you wanted to find a piece of stamp to complete a set, it would be so much challenging than today. Mr. Google is always so kind to tell you where to find what you want. So, don't let him sit down there doing nothing while he can bring you so much values

✓ Actively promote China stamps!!! If you want your assets to appreciate in value, chip in your efforts to make it more popular. Each of us can be a catalyst to make our assets more valuable

✓ Beware of forgeries. The more popular China stamps become, the more often forgeries are being come across. Learn as much as possible from different resources, and most importantly from your knowledgeable network to get yourself ready to detect and stay away from forgeries. Things take time. You just need to be patient and enhance your knowledge every day

✓ Seek consultation from the experts if you are venturing into investment. This is very important since you are going to deal with five figures worth of capital

Don'ts

✗ Don't collect or invest in any expensive items if you don't know much about the subject matters. Doing so is just like gambling

✗ Don't overpay for any stamps. Study the stamps carefully before you accept any offers by sellers. I have ever seen newbies paying $60 for a coiling dragon stamp while the real value of the stamp is just a few dollars. Don't be the victim of ignorance. Keep learning a little bit every day if you are serious in collecting

✗ Don't be distracted by so many options in the market. Define a scope for yourself and follow your plan. You can't have everything. Don't be controlled by greed and burst your budget or one day you find yourself overloaded and decide to give up

✗ Don't transact only by looking at the catalogue value. Pay attention to the condition as well. A lot of people are still making this mistake and wasting their money on average quality items

✗ Don't go into buying and selling for quick profits. It won't give you any good margin in the short-term. If you think you can impose a high mark-up, be very careful! One day if your buyers become more experienced, you'll get into big troubles

✗ Don't speculate. Although China stamps are highly popular, it doesn't mean they won't devaluate. Let's learn from the lessons of the stock and real estate bubbles in the past, and avoid the same thing happening to collectibles. I'm sure you don't want to wake up one day and become the owner of thousands of worthless little pieces of paper. Many people are, in fact, speculating Zodiac stamps. Let's make sure you're not one of them!!!

✗ Don't collect if money is your only motivation. When you're not driven by passion, chances are that you won't make extra efforts to preserve the stamps and enhance the value of your collection. You'll get frustrated upon seeing your stamps monetizing at lower rate and slower pace than expected

✗ Last but not least, don't keep stamps if you can't manage to take care of them. Degraded stamps are much less valuable than well-preserved stamps

I want to conclude this book with an interesting point about collectors and investors. You would agree with me that most investors are driven by monetary factors. They focus on value, growth and how their bottom-line looks like. They care less about the stamps' design and historical implications. Collectors, on the other hand, would pay more attention to the stamps themselves before talking about catalogue values. To them, catalogue might not reflect the whole picture. Though each stamp has a value being assigned in the catalogue, it might be perceived differently by different collectors. An average-priced stamp would mean a lot to you if the event it features had significant impact on you and your family; or it was given to you by an important person of your life. On the contrary, an expensive stamp that brings back tragic memory to you would never be allocated a space in your album.

Stamp collecting is just an extraordinary exciting hobby! I hope you enjoy the content of this book, and will continue to support my future projects. Please feel free to follow the content of my Facebook page for interesting sharing:
https://www.facebook.com/richardtangphilately

Last but not least, I hope you can do me a favor by leaving a positive review for this book.

All the best to your stamp collecting journey!

November 2017
Richard Tang

Richard Tang

Made in the USA
Middletown, DE
02 September 2024